THE JOURNAL

*When Ordinary People
Get Extraordinary Information*

by

**SUZANNE LIE, PH.D.
www.multidimensions.com**

INTRODUCTION
~Lisa Finds the Journal~

~ LISA ~

"I have been trying to contact my mother for two weeks," said Lisa to herself as she slammed down the phone.

"What is she up to now?" Lisa muttered to herself. "I guess I will have to go down there and find out for myself. That means I have to have another confrontation with Bruce about my 'weird' mother.

"The kids are in school, so I will have to get someone to pick them up and watch them until Bruce comes home. What a bother!!" Lisa continued her inner dialogue, or was she talking out loud?

"Why doesn't she just communicate with me? I know we have not seen eye-to-eye for a while, but a little communication on her end would greatly help our relationship. That is if we even have a relationship," Lisa said so loudly that she knew she was talking aloud to herself.

What else was she to do? She certainly could not get in contact with her mother. Truth be told, she had not tried that hard to contact her until recently. Her mother had been talking about so much weird stuff lately that Lisa had found herself avoiding contacting her.

Then, when she finally did call, her mother did not answer. Not her phone, not her emails, and not her Skype. Her mother was nowhere to be found. "Bruce is going to be so upset about this," Lisa said to herself. "He has really had it with my 'crazy mother,' as he likes to call her."

Lisa tried for two more days to connect with her mother. Finally, she could wait no longer. She confronted Bruce, got the babysitter, and left at 5:00 a.m. for the journey to her mother's house. She told Bruce she was leaving then to avoid traffic, but she really wanted to avoid another confrontation with him and the many questions from the children.

For the same reason she slept in the guestroom and told Bruce it was so that she would not wake him up. Actually, she did not want to "sleep" with him. Sex had been a chore for ages now, and the more she disliked it, the more often he seemed to want it.

If Lisa could tell herself the truth, which she had been avoiding for a very long time, she was very unhappy in her marriage and needed to talk to her weird, but loving, mother. If Lisa could tell herself the truth, she would have to admit that her best friend was far too close with her husband.

Since she could not even admit that much, she could more easily look past all the obvious signs of Bruce's wandering eye. "No," Lisa yelled, as she pushed aside the obvious evidence and chose to live the lie. However, four hours of driving alone in a car would make it very difficult to ignore herself.

By the time she arrived at her mother's house, she was enraged, in tears and so relieved to be in a safe environment. However, it was an empty environment. The house was neat and clean as always, but the plants were gone, the cat was missing and the house felt empty of all life.

No mother, no copious plants, no cat, windows closed and all doors locked. The yard was a bit overgrown, but watered by the sprinklers. The refrigerator was filled with expired food and the bread in the pantry was covered with mold. Now Lisa was getting worried.

She had spoken to her mother so seldom lately, that she did not even know how to contact her mother's friends. That was if she had any. Truth be told, Lisa was glad when her husband took the job up north and they had to move away. She did not understand her mother at all. Now her mother had disappeared, just when Lisa was finally ready to talk with her.

"How could she just disappear?" yelled Lisa after she had searched every area of the house and yard. The car was in the garage and her mother's purse with her wallet inside was by her bed, which showed no sign of recent occupancy. Perhaps there was a clue in her office, where she shut herself up for hours to meditate or write or whatever she did, thought Lisa as she walked to the back of the house.

Lisa had been embarrassed by her mother's behavior as a teenager and had never brought her friends over. Lisa was more like her father, who had left them because her mother was so odd. Now her mother was causing problems with Lisa's marriage. Perhaps the answer was in her office, Lisa thought as she went into that room.

When Lisa opened the door to enter the office, she felt a sudden chill. What was that saying? Like someone had walked over a grave. "Oh my God," Lisa said out loud. "What if she *is* dead?"

Fortunately, there was no dead body and *no* mother. The room was neat, much neater than Lisa had seen it in a long time. In fact, her mother's desk, which was often a mess of papers, was totally clear except for a large three-ring folder filled almost to the breaking point.

As Lisa tentatively walked to the desk, she saw an envelope with her name on it taped to the top of the folder. She angrily pulled off the envelope, opened it and began to read her mother's note.

~ BEVERLY'S JOURNAL~

My dear Lisa, I am so sorry that I was unable to tell you this in person, but there was too much to say and too little time in which to say it. Therefore, I have left this journal, which describes what has been occurring in my life.

I wish that I could have shared it with you, but you have made it very clear that you do not want to hear about my "weird" encounters with what you call "the unknown." I have tried to tell you that it was *never* unknown to me, but when I did you became angry.

I know that you have blamed my behavior for your father leaving us when you were only ten, but I did not want him to leave any more than you did. I also know that I was an embarrassment to you when you were a teenager. I am sorry that I was not the person that you needed me to be.

Mostly, I am sorry that I could never find a way to share my experiences with you that did not upset or anger you. I hope that you find this journal in which I recount everything that has been happening in my life in the order in which it occurred. Perhaps, when you read it within your own time, you can begin to understand why I have disappeared in this manner.

Please remember that I love you very much and hope that we can regain our relationship. Please do not run off to phone the police before you read the entire journal. After you have read it, we may even be able to communicate with each other again.

I love you,
Mom

~LISA~

"What," yelled Lisa. "Do you expect me to read this whole silly journal before I call the police to find out where you are?"

Lisa was so angry that she violently pushed the journal off the table, where it fell to the floor, opening the binder and spilling the pages all over the room. Lisa stood in horror. She finally found a clue as to her mother's disappearance and she had just scattered it all over the floor. She was so upset that she fell into the nearby chair and sobbed.

Lisa cried the tears that she would not allow when she saw the look in her husband's eye when her friend came over, or how her "friend" looked toward the ground. She cried the tears that she had pushed away during her four-hour drive here alone. Then, when she remembered the expression of relief she saw on her husband's face when she said she needed to leave town, she became almost hysterical.

She needed her mother to talk to *now*. But was she there for her? *No!* Again, she was absorbed in her own self and in her own weird whatever she was involved in. How could her mother leave this silly book instead of calling her and talking to her? But that question reminded Lisa that she had not taken a phone call from her mother for quite a while.

She had been "busy" and said she would call her back, but never did. Lisa told herself that it was because she was fed up with her mother's ideas. But the truth was that her mother could always read her mind, and she hadn't wanted her mother to tell her what she wasn't ready to face.

During her four hours driving alone in the car she had "unconsciously" decided to talk to her mother about her marriage. She was even ready to ask for her help. "But NO," Lisa yelled to the empty room. "I finally am ready to talk to her and Mom is involved in her own self—again!"

Lisa dramatically fell to the floor and sobbed. She cried because her marriage was over, her life was a mess, her mother was missing and she was totally alone. However, being alone was what she really craved. She needed to get out of denial and into the truth. That was the real reason she had driven to her mother's.

However, her mother was not there, and had not been there for a while. Maybe she should have answered some of her mother's phone calls, emails and letters. Maybe she should have just listened to herself, Lisa thought as the tears were spent and she sat on the floor and looked at the papers strewn all over the room.

It took Lisa an hour to collect all the pages, which fortunately were numbered, and put them back into the folder. By then she had calmed down. She went to the kitchen and happily found some coffee, sat down at the kitchen table, where she had often done her homework as a child, and began to read the journal.

PART I

I
THE JOURNAL
~Beverly's Secret~

~BEVERLY'S JOURNAL~

Dear Journal,

I look around my room and see that it is filled with thought forms. This is my meditation room where I write, draw, meditate, and engage in my ongoing search for higher dimensional realities. I have uncovered quite a few higher dimensional lives, as well as some lower dimensional lives that were not very enjoyable.

However, my inner guidance told me to stay with them all, higher and lower until they told me their full story. You see, I have been coming to this planet since Gaia asked for assistance during the fall of Atlantis. The darkness had overtaken Her planetary body and Earth was falling off its axis.

Therefore I, and many others, each forced (and I do mean forced) our expanded consciousness into one of the many dying ones at the time of the demise of Atlantis. We volunteered to do so because we had offered to bring our multidimensional light to assist Gaia. Earth did maintain its integrity, barely, but Gaia's dimensional fall landed in the lower third dimension.

The third-dimensional frequency of reality was so deeply polarized that for myriad incarnations most of us, including myself, became lost in the illusions of that lower dimension of reality. Fortunately, it is the NOW for personal and planetary awakening.

The forces of darkness are quite aware of that fact and trying everything they can to scare us back into subservience. It is for this reason that I am writing this journal. I intend to publish it, or maybe put it up on the Internet.

I am not sure what the future holds for me, which is why I must take a long look at what I have considered to be my past. You see, Gaia is now expanding Her frequency into the higher dimensions from which She has fallen. She has waited as long as She can for humanity. Her elementals are ready, Her plants are ready and Her animals are ready.

However, the very thing that made humanity the most powerful species on the planet is the exact thing that is causing our demise. I wish that I could identify exactly what that "thing" is, but I cannot. Therefore, I am going to combine all that I have learned from as many incarnations and realities that my 3D brain can access.

Of course, I am no longer limited to my 3D brain, as many decades of meditation, prayer and believing my "imagination" have opened my awareness to perceptions beyond my physical reality. These perceptions have finally brought me to the first real peace I can remember, but they have also isolated me from almost everyone I know.

I hope that someday my daughter may read this journal, which is why I am leaving it on my desk in the office. If anyone cares enough to find out what happed to me, it would be her. The reality is, I am not even sure what happened to me. I know that I am jumping back and forth in time from starting the journal to ending the journal, but that is, indeed, my life.

Since I feel that I am at the ending, though I am not sure what is ending, I need to go back to the beginning, which has to be my childhood. There are myriad realities that surround us in every moment of our day. They can all be entered via the many floating thought forms of which I have spoken.

We have forgotten that our consciousness is the key to open the doorway into any reality that we choose. In fact, most of us forgot that there were myriad realities. As children, these inner realities were acceptable as they were "just our imagination." But as we became adults, we had to push away those other realities because the physical reality we were living was overwhelming.

Besides, only "crazy" people could see and interact with other realities. Therefore, we forgot that we could choose our reality. We bought the lies we were fed by those who sought to control and possess rather than to love and create.

We tried to control our life so that "they" would not control us. However, control in any manner is a trap, as we cannot control and surrender at the same time. Control is the mechanism of the third dimension, whereas surrender opens the pathway into the higher worlds.

Therefore, by controlling our lives, we see only third-dimensional options and solutions for our third-dimensional situations. These options were not enough for me, but I am getting out of sequence again. I need to go back to the beginning, my childhood, and write this journal in some form of time-bound sequence, or no one will understand it.

~LISA~

"You are so right, Mom," cried Lisa. "Already I don't understand you. And where the heck are you?" yelled Lisa, not meaning to shout. "I drove four hours down here to talk to you in person and what I get is a journal. My kids are with their father, who can only take my absence for so long. Besides he will run out of all the food I left them.

"Where are you? I had a huge fight with my husband to come down here and had to go into my savings to get help for the kids. How could you be so selfish? I know we were close when I was young, being an only child and all. However, as soon as I stopped believing in all your weirdo stuff, we started growing apart."

Lisa was very angry, but there was a bit of fear in her voice as well. Unconsciously recognizing the fear, Lisa went back to her reading in hopes of finding a clue about her mother. She took a few more sips of coffee and returned to her reading.

~BEVERLY'S JOURNAL~

You might say that I was a very imaginative child. In fact, I lived in my imagination so much that sometimes I got confused about what world was the real world. That is when I saw the floating thought forms. I did not know that they were thought forms. To my childhood reality, these moments of communicating with another reality were more real than my daily life.

In my daily life I was just a normal kid who was not too smart, too pretty, too clever or too anything. But when unseen portals inside my mind suddenly, or slowly, opened, I was no longer a child. I was a Native American riding across the planes on a pinto pony. I was a young boy crossing America in a covered wagon. I was a Priestess in a far off place called Atlantis, or a young man navigating a spaceship.

All these thought forms floated around me. All I needed to "do" to enter a thought form was to allow my thoughts and feelings to flow into that world by feeling the emotions of that "me" and thinking the thoughts of "that" me. Of course, as a child I did not know it was a thought form. I had no idea what "IT" was, but as a child I did not care.

In fact, it felt like if I told anyone about what I was experiencing that my secret portal would close and I would be "cast adrift on a hostile planet." I know that statement sounds extreme, but it was exactly how I felt. If they ever talked about therapy at that time, I would have been there. That is, of course, if I ever told anyone about my secret life, which I never did.

Fortunately, there was this flowing, cloud presence that was always with me when I entered these worlds that told me not to tell anyone about what I was doing. The sparkling cloud being was too big to be a thought form and it felt different. This presence was not like the thought form that became a portal if I opened and entered it. I did not enter the floating cloud being, but it *did* enter me.

When the floating being entered me I felt so very wonderful, pure, honest, invincible and secure. But, it did not enter me very often. It usually just guided me and helped me to enter, what it called the "thought forms." My cloud friend taught me that if I could believe in myself, by entering a thought form I would enable it to become a portal to another world.

All that "imagination" and floating friends were fine when I was a child, but when I was a teenager I began to change. I no longer wanted to play with my floating friend and enter the wonderful portals that it presented to me as thought forms. I was becoming a woman and needed a boyfriend to prove it. And so, my floating friend was put aside, like an old doll I had loved as a child.

I was too old for all that imagination stuff. So, I stopped attending to the floating thought forms and ignored my cloud friend. After all, they were only for children, and I was growing up. That is exactly when I became VERY depressed! That depression followed me for many years of my life.

I forgot about floating thought forms and, too often, I forgot about my cloud friend. I was becoming an adult and had to behave accordingly. But enough of becoming an adult; I have said I would begin with my childhood, and so I will.

Beverly

~LISA~

Lisa closed the Journal in a state of mind that she could not identify. She wanted to be angry, but instead she felt sad. Yes, it was her mother's life that made her sad. Her life was fine, in fact it was happy. The only problem was that she had to come all the way down here to find out where her wacky mother was.

Well, maybe her mother wasn't too wacky. Maybe Lisa just thought that because she was so angry with her for not being there. In fact, for not being there too many times when she needed someone to talk to. But with that thought Lisa began to realize that she had not talked to her mother in a long time.

"Too much thinking on an empty stomach and no sleep," Lisa said to herself. She should call her husband and tell him that she had arrived safely, but she didn't. She did not want to think about why she didn't call him, but she did call her friend who the kids were staying with while her husband was at work.

She pushed the journal aside, stood up and opened the refrigerator to find some food. She did *not* want to continue with that line of thought. She found some food in the freezer, which was OK and made more coffee. However, after she finally ate, even the coffee could not keep her awake.

Therefore, Lisa went over to the couch to lie down for "just a few minutes." She woke up hours later. "Wow, what a dream," she said to herself when she awoke. Fortunately, she soon forgot it.

Lisa took a long bath in her mother's huge tub. Then she got dressed to go to a restaurant for a decent meal. She was about to step out the door when she went back into the kitchen and got the journal. After all, it was cozy to read something while eating at a restaurant.

II
THE JOURNAL
~Meeting Mytria~

~LISA~

Lisa drove to a restaurant she seldom went to, but knew it had nice tables with little cubbyhole areas. The last thing she wanted was to meet someone she knew. She ordered her meal and some tea, as she could not take any more coffee, and decided she would scan the Journal while she waited for her food. She opened the journal to the page where she had left off before leaving the house. When she scanned the next section, she discovered it was about finding Mytria.

~BEVERLY'S JOURNAL~

Dear Journal,

I am happy to announce that my "cloud friend" finally did return. It was a long process, which I will recount in this journal. I am telling you of the long-awaited reconnection with my unseen friend, that I now know as "the Arcturian," as it is only because of that ongoing support that I am able to write this journal.

I believe that it is important that I share my

experiences with others now because our ever expanding consciousness manifests our thoughts and feelings almost instantly. Therefore, if we think we are having anxiety or an illness, then that is our reality. On the other hand, if we think we are having symptoms of awakening, then that is our reality.

There are, of course, times when we are sick or injured. Those times come when there are old emotions or memories that need to be purged. Therefore, we create a certain scenario in which we have to be still and center our attention on our SELF, so that we can complete this purge.

Since I have been feeling "sick" for quite a while now, I know it is the NOW to tell my story. Also, last night I had a dream in which I connected with a deep, deep fear from my childhood that it is time to release. Again, I hope I don't offend anyone by my admission, but it is my truth, and I vowed to speak only my truth here. Also, I know that I am not the only one who has had these experiences.

When I was a child my imagination took me into many of my alternate realities, often known as "past" lives. These adventures stopped as a teenager, but returned when I started working with my first spiritual teacher. For many years, my adventures were earthbound and included many different eras in which I was male or female.

As an adult, I began to have visitations/imaginations off-world and on other planets. First it was Venus.

Then I began to hear from Mytria in the Pleiades. I know that I could have had an awakened experience of visiting a spaceship, but I felt a submerged fear at the prospect whenever I imagined it.

Through my adventures on Venus and with Mytria, I came to realize that fear of visiting a spaceship was because I was abducted by one as a young teenager. I further remembered that my abductors, the Zetas, placed a small implant into my brain to make me fear spaceships and make me too afraid to tell anyone about my experience.

Of course, telling people was not a problem for me, as I had learned long ago that I could not tell people about my dreams or psychic experiences. Plus, there is not a lot I can say about my abduction, anyway, as I have yet to recover most of the details.

My dream last night also told me that my wounded child needed my attention, and I had to heal her before I could go on to the next level of my awakening. In that dream, I felt the terror of my disconnection from my sleeping physical self and my desperation to return to my sleeping body. I woke up knowing that I had to address the issue of my wounded, abducted, inner child/teen.

I remember very little about those experiences. I clearly remember lying on the cold metal table with faces looking down at me. I remember sharp things, too many sharp things. I am well into my adulthood and I have never had any surgery at all, and I hate going to the dentist.

I also know exactly where my implant is, and I can feel the fear right now as I share this. The Arcturians told me this morning that the implant leaves an embedded message to never share what has happened. Maybe I can't share the experience, or even remember it precisely, but I can still share my journey of processing and releasing my fears, all of them, including this deep-seated, alien-implanted one from my childhood.

I see writing this journal as a conscious action that shows that I AM ready to clear my old fears so that I can contribute my full love and light to this planetary awakening into truth! I KNOW I want to communicate with the Arcturians on their Ship in my fully conscious mind. Therefore, I am committed to completing this process of sharing my experiences and the messages I have received with others. However, I do not know if anyone else will be able to believe that the experiences I am about to recount could possibly be true.

Nevertheless, I will tell my story, if only to bring clarity into my own life. Perhaps some of the people I love will be able to still accept and love me, but I fear that most of them will not. Hence, even though I write this journal, I may need to send it out under a false name. On the other hand, perhaps if they read what I have experienced in my life, they may learn to accept me more.

~LISA~

"Is that a challenge, Mom?" Lisa muttered into her tea. However, with the bath and some good food, she was feeling better and had to admit how angry she had been at her mother. "What did she actually do to me, that is other than believe in different things than I did?" said Lisa, continuing to soften. Lisa ordered some dessert, and continued her reading as she waited for it to arrive.

~BEVERLY'S JOURNAL~

In about 1995, I began to receive inner messages from a female Pleiadian. I had heard about the Pleiadians somewhere, and since I had begun to remember my childhood abduction, I was looking for a kinder, gentler alien. The Pleiadians are tall, blond, and very attractive. They also look very human. Therefore, I asked my inner channels if I could speak to a Pleiadian, and I received the name "Mytria."

Before I continue, perhaps I should explain about what I mean by my "inner channels." I grew up going to church, and then was in a teen church group, so speaking to unseen higher beings was not an unusual event. In fact, when I was a child I often talked to my cloud being and called him Jesus. I continued those conversations into my teens—for a while.

When I was young, I called what I do to connect with other beings "praying." When I became an adult and went to many spiritual teachers and meditation classes, I called it "meditating." I knew that many people did not get the in-depth answers that I got, but maybe that was because they did not write down what they were experiencing.

Long story short, I now add the first dates and messages I received through Mytria:

~BEVERLY'S JOURNAL~

11-20-95

Dear Mytria,

I have asked to speak with a Pleaidian and I received your name. I am opening myself to your reply, as I wish to speak with you. I hope that I have been able to clear myself enough so that I can have a clear reception of your message.
Beverly

I was very surprised to receive this response:

Dear Beverly,

You have indeed been opening yourself to me and, in doing so, you can consciously receive messages from a higher dimensional being such as myself. I am from Alcoyne and I am one of the Guardians of the Sacred

Fire. I speak to you now from the fifth dimension, although I could also communicate with you from higher dimensions. Since this is our first contact, I will take on my lowest vibration to make it easier for you to understand me.

Even though I am the Guardian of the Sacred Flame, there is no need to guard the Flame from danger in our world, as no one here would damage anything. Beings on the fifth dimension know that any action affects them as much as those around them. You too are learning that lesson. Hence, I amend my statement to say it would be more correct to say that I assist those who wish to enter the Violet Fire.

The Sacred Fire is a portal through which one can pass to travel to anywhere in the Multiverse. In our fifth-dimensional Pleiadian world, we can step into and out of our body as easily as you would step in or out of your dress. You see, our bodies can be easily transmuted to a higher dimension by returning to pure spirit to travel into another dimension.

Spiritual explorers will come to the Sacred Fire, and leave their bodies there while they travel in spirit. When they return from their travels, they project their essence into the Sacred Fire to return to their body. While their body is in the Sacred Flame they can safely travel via their consciousness to any place they desire."

I am one of the Pleiadian Priestesses who oversee that process. Therefore, I guess it would be better to say that I guard the body of the traveler rather than the

Flame. However, our title is 'Keeper of the Flame.' You, my dear, have contacted me because I am open to communications with those from other dimensions, and because I know you.

In fact, you might say that I am a higher frequency of the physical you. This is why you have always had such a strong urge to reach beyond your mundane world. Indeed, when you merge with the higher frequency expressions of yourself, you will be able to communicate with as many higher beings as you wish.

Do you understand now how your entire life has been in preparation for that service?

~LISA~

"Whoa, Mom, I was starting to follow your book, but this is just over the top," Lisa accidently said out loud, as she pushed the journal away, almost spilling her tea. Trying to think the words rather than say them, she thought, "No wonder Dad left you. If he even got a hint of this type of thinking he would have put you in the loony bin."

This time Lisa did not even try to understand her mother, who was obviously delusional. She opened her purse to get the cash for dinner and left the table in a rush.

"Miss," she heard behind her. "You left your book." The young waitress smiled sweetly as she brought the book to Lisa, who tried to smile and muttered, "Thanks." Lisa did not know what was worse, that she had to take the crazy book or that the waitress had called her "miss."

Lisa was starting to tear up again. Just when she thought she would maybe go to her mother for help with her life, she found this journal with this psycho writing. Walking as fast as she could to the car, Lisa rummaged for the car keys and almost dropped the book in the mud while doing so.

She was very surprised that she chose to drop the keys rather than the journal. "Oh my God," she thought. "I hope this stuff isn't contagious." She had to smile as she clicked the key to unlock the car, threw the stupid journal in the back seat, put on her seatbelt and drove back to her mother's empty house.

Fortunately the electricity was still on, as it was dark by the time she got to the house. Lisa parked the car in the driveway and got out. To her surprise, she opened the back door and retrieved the journal, as she muttered, "Well, there is nothing else to do here. Besides, maybe if I read this thing I will find out where she is."

Lisa pushed aside the distant fear that her mother was dead or lost or had suffered some foul play. "Now I am being as silly as Mom," Lisa said as she opened the front door, turned on the light and went to the bedroom to change her clothes. She knew that there would not be too much sleep. Just in case there was something besides silly stories, she knew that she had to read that Journal.

Once Lisa had put on some lights, the heater, and changed into her PJs, she got a glass of wine and sat on her favorite chair to read. This chair had been where she often did her homework before she went away to college. Her mother had left it just the way it was, even though she had changed some of the other furniture.

"Does that mean she was waiting for me to visit?" she thought with more than a bit of guilt as she opened the book. She braced herself to hear more about the Pleiadian woman who was the "Keeper of the Flame."

~BEVERLY'S JOURNAL~

Mytria's message continued:

The merging of your alternate selves begins by communicating with them.

~LISA~

"I would rather 'merge' with my mother," Lisa muttered as she took a sip of wine. Maybe she should get the bottle? She might need to be a bit drunk to understand this nonsense. She returned to Mytria's message.

~BEVERLY'S JOURNAL~

Do you see Kepier with me now? Kepier and I are sisters in the Light. I have studied on Arcturus, where she is from, and she has studied on Alycone. Dear Beverly, take a moment of your time to realize how it feels to be able to move from galaxy to galaxy with less effort that it takes for you to drive to the grocery store.

~LISA~

Lisa rolled her eyes, but continued. That is, she continued after she took a long drink of wine.

~BEVERLY'S JOURNAL~

Kepier is appearing very female here even though she is androgynous, because the vibration of our planet is so feminine. When she is on Arcturus, she appears quite differently and looks like your Arcturian "cloud friend."

I will now tell you some things about our life here in the Pleiades. We live very simply in large open central homes and smaller sleeping/meditation quarters. The time for sleeping is not like it is on Earth. Here we remain totally conscious, and what you would call sleep, we call meditation. Therefore, it is better if we are alone, because we go deeply into our consciousness to expand our awareness and then integrate what we have learned into our daily lives.

We also use our quarters for merging with our mates, if we have chosen to take one. Some here wish to live with their Divine Complements as man and woman, and others wish to integrate their two components and live as one androgynous being. It is purely a matter of choice on this dimension. On higher dimensions, the division of genders is unknown.

We receive our children from the Flame as is done on Venus, but some still wish to have the experience of pregnancy and child birth. When I say 'we' receive our young from the Flame, I mean that 'we' as a male and female Divine Compliment couple, or 'we' as one androgynous being.

Either way, we meditate and train for what would be years of your time to prepare for the great honor of being a parent. Only couples that are Divine Compliments parent together. When our teachers have told us that our vibration has reached a beautiful silver-violet shade, we go into the Flame with our Divine Complement (or as a unified androgynous being).

When we are standing before the Violet Flame, we call into the higher dimensions to see if a Spirit wishes to take a life in our world. Once a Spirit has decided to choose the experience of incarnation into the fifth dimension of Pleiades, the parents and Spirit work together to begin the process of what you would call "birth."

Together the parents and child determine if it is best for them all to remain in the Flame until the Spirit is ready to take a life in their Pleiadian world, or for the Spirit to enter into the female and go through a pregnancy, much like on your Earth. Here, however, the male and female are equally involved in the pregnancy.

The male must move up and down the Flame regularly so that the Spirit can pull enough of its essence into the fifth dimension to create and inhabit a form. On the other hand, the female must stay away from the Flame, as she is the grounding force for the new life.

When the male returns from the Flame, holding the essence of the Spirit, he places it on the woman's womb to offer the fetus the love of a mother. The man then embraces both the mother and child, as both parents send their child unconditional love and infinite peace. The three remain intertwined until the Spirit of the child can gradually adapt to our fifth-dimensional reality.

If this form of "pregnancy" is not chosen, the couple or the androgynous being must live near, and move in and out of the Flame, until the Spirit is ready to create itself a fifth-dimensional form. Once the Spirit is an 'infant' he, she, or an androgynous self (children can be born androgynous here) will move with the parent, or unified parent, to the Central Living Room.

The Central Living Room is the living area where our "greater family" lives. The word we use for this room is difficult to hear in English. It sounds like "scrdala." The scrdala is comprised of members of the same Oversoul. On the seventh dimension, the Oversoul is one being. As new 'children' of our society move into the lower dimensions, the Oversoul guards over its fifth-dimensional fragment while it makes its descent to the lower realms via the Violet Flame.

Each of these fragments remain in constant contact with their sixth-dimensional self in the Violet Flame until their new form can contain their great life force. The parents keep their "infant" in constant connection with the mother, father, or both of them to assist their child in grounding his or her consciousness in the lower frequency.

The members of the "greater family" of new parents, who are also temporarily living in the scrdala, work in unity to assist the new members of our Pleiadian reality to acclimate to their new life. This group is more than a family, as they function as ONE being of parental love who are welcoming new life into our world.

When each family leaves the scrdala, the choices of living situations differ with the frequency to which they resonate. A being who is able to be awake on many different vibrations at once, such as myself, will have very different situations on each plane. This is much like your situation.

On the third dimension, you live a quiet, private life. On the fourth dimension, you live in Faerie with your beloved fairies and Nature creatures, and on the fifth dimension you are me! Yes, dear, you and I are ONE.

We are different expressions of the same Oversoul, the same Being. Kepier is another fifth-dimensional expression of our being. IlliaEm is an eighth-dimensional expression of our Oversoul.

There are also many other expressions of our Oversoul that you have not met yet, however, you soon will. It is this way for ALL the grounded ones on Earth. All of you have octaves of your SELF that are expressed in myriad times, worlds, and dimensions. Because you are incarnated on ascending Earth, your multidimensional consciousness has split into myriad expressions in preparation for your grounding into developing fifth-dimensional planet.

On the sixth dimension, you are on Venus, where you are able to visit and communicate with your Pleiadian and Antarian expressions of SELF. Your Arcturian self resonates to the eighth through tenth dimensions and can move between myriad locations because you are not in need of a planetary Home. Your sixth-dimensional self travels often to Antares as well as to Arcturus, Sirius, or here in the Pleiades.

I can see your mental question about whether or not these different portions of your SELF ever meet. The answer is, of course! Are we not doing that now? However, each SELF is also a different reality. Much like the different realities you have experienced and remembered in your third-dimensional self. In the physical world these portions of your self are separated by time and space. On the other dimensions, the different selves or realities resonate to different vibrations.

~LISA~

"OK," scoffed Lisa, "That is enough for me. Enough of this book and enough of this wine! I am not sure if I am more upset about the book or about the fact that Mom left me without saying a word."

However, she did have to admit that there had been quite a few calls from her mother that she had been too "busy" to return. But, she was not ready to take responsibility for anything yet. She could not even admit that she was so very happy to be away from her house, her husband and even the kids.

What was wrong with her lately? She felt kind of empty inside, as though she just did not have any more to give. So she came to her mother's house to get something and her mother was gone! Lisa slammed the empty wine glass onto the table, almost breaking it, allowed the journal to fall on the floor and went into her mother's guestroom to get some sleep.

She tried not to wonder why she remembered to pick up the journal and take it with her.

Lisa woke up at 10:00 a.m. Oh, what kind of Heaven was that? However, as soon as she sat up and felt her headache, Heaven was over. Even though she had a splitting head, she had a strange sense of peace and calm about her. Then, with a start, she realized that she had not called the kids, or her husband, or her friend who was helping with the kids.

She had been angry at her mother for not communicating with her, and she had done the same thing to her own children. "Like mother, like daughter," she said as she reached for her phone, which was out of juice. Then she had to look through her luggage. "Oh please, please, I DID remember to bring the cord," she said to herself.

Fortunately, the cord was found, the phone plugged in, and to her surprise, she did NOT call her husband first. NO, she called her friend first and found out that she was the saint she had always been and had fed all the kids, her own and Lisa's, and taken them to school. Continuing with her saintly behavior, she did not even ask Lisa when she would be home.

Lisa was so happy that she did not have to lie to such a great friend. However, she could not tell her friend the truth because she did not know it. "Oh, yes Cindy, my mother has completely disappeared and I am reading her journal about her Pleiadian self." Nor could she tell Cindy that she was so happy to be alone for a while. There was something she had to figure out, that was, besides the whereabouts of her missing mother.

Why hadn't she phoned the police? How did she know that her mother was OK? The cat had a home, the electricity and sprinklers were on and the phones still worked. She could not have been gone too long, or all that would have been turned off. But, why didn't her mother tell her where she was. Oh yes, the ignored phone calls.

After a long, hot shower and more coffee, she returned to Mytria. Of course, she would have to go to the store, call her mother's friends, if she could find her mom's phonebook and, oh yes, call her husband. But he had not called her, so why did she need to call him? However, she did remember to NOT look at her missed phone calls. Her kids were fine, and Cindy and Bruce were taking care of them.

After the shower and coffee, she was ready for the journal, which happened to be right next to her bed. With coffee in hand, she grabbed the journal and returned to her "high school homework chair" to see what else Mytria had to say.

~BEVERLY'S JOURNAL~

Mytria's message continued:

Each reality, or life, is separate until you are able to become conscious of it, then it is a portion of the whole. Your perception of the "whole" increases as your consciousness expands.

Furthermore, each component of your self can be individual within the unity of your Multidimensional

SELF. We Pleiadians often wish to keep our "fragments" individuated so that we can explore each reality with depth and intimacy.

I, Mytria, am able to raise my vibration to the seventh dimension where I can communicate with all the other aspects of my SELF. Each of us is individual as well as ONE. Of course, this scenario is only possible when our bodies resonate beyond time and space.

~LISA~

"What?" questioned Lisa, not quite as snarly as she would have asked the day before. Something was bothering her. Yes, it was a dream. She could not remember the dream, but the feeling of it troubled her. She shrugged it off and returned to the text.

~BEVERLY'S JOURNAL~

I wish now to answer your thought about why it took you so long to feel my presence. Your connection to me was difficult to feel because it begins on the fifth dimension, and your consciousness can only expand to that frequency when you are calm and meditative.

Also if you were to communicate with me before this time, it would have been too confusing to you. Do you see how much difficulty you had even now with some of the concepts that I have presented to you?

~LISA~

"Yes," Lisa replied without noticing. This time her reply was not angry. Maybe that was because of her dream.

~BEVERLY'S JOURNAL~

It is good that you are stretching your imagination and consciousness to embrace what will soon come into your world. Most of all, the Goddess, Mother Earth, Gaia is awakening. She will soon hear the mating call of Her Divine Complement and will no longer tolerate any injustice to Her being.

Gaia will be a bride preparing for her wedding. She will make herself beautiful, and anyone who tries to stop Her will not enjoy the consequences. It will be a wonderful time. You, and others like you, will at last be happy to be born on Earth in a third-dimensional form.

Then, because you all will learn to totally love life on the third dimension, you will be able to release that life. You will not need to release your form, of course, but you will release all of its limitations and separations. Your physical body will be like the car you drive on Earth, as it will hold your consciousness. Then, when you wish a new, improved "vehicle," for your consciousness, you will easily replace the old one.

Only, you will NOT have to take out a loan. You will create, free and clear, the vehicle of your choice.

I look forward to many more communications with you, and I await your next visit to my world.

Mytria

~LISA~

Lisa did not understand why she did not get angry like she did before. But, it was nice to not feel angry for a minute. In fact, when she was NOT angry, she began to understand how angry she had been.

No, the anger was not about her mother. It wasn't even because of her husband. She was angry because something was missing, and she did not know what. She almost felt good, until her mother moved on to UFOs.

~BEVERLY'S JOURNAL~

1-26-96

Dear Mytria,

I would like a quick word from you regarding my UFO search. I spent many hours trying to find some information and all I found was information about the Zetas.

Beverly

Dear Beverly,

There are actually few humans who can take the leap of communicating with us in this fashion, which is why there is so little information about us and our Starship. To do something alone without the support of others to validate your experience is not something that many people are brave enough to do.

However, you have felt alone inside yourself your entire life. You have always kept secrets from others because you had learned that it was not safe to share what you knew inside yourself. Now you are getting strong enough to begin to share your knowledge. However, there is a certain amount of preparation of yourself that must take place before you can go "public" with your information.

When you are ready to be totally open with what you know, you will find others who are doing the same thing. We Pleiadians are communicating with quite a few people. However, it will be a while yet before you can speak with each other through your Internet. People still need a certain amount of proof to validate their experiences. Do not be concerned. We are here with you.

Mytria

~LISA~

To her surprise, Lisa continued reading. There was something about this Mytria person that felt, well, it felt familiar. However, she could not tell anyone that. They would think she was crazy. Lisa continued reading. She didn't even get up to get more coffee.

~BEVERLY'S JOURNAL~

3-10-96

Dear Mytria,

Do you have a message for me today?

Beverly

Dearest Beverly,

I am glad to see that you are coming to peace with your third and fourth-dimensional experiences. Forgiveness of others and yourself is indeed the key, as forgiveness is the energy field that allows you to release that which has reached its completion. Your feelings of aloneness and competition are part of this process of transmutation.

First you had to feel and release the sadness of the ages. This sadness is an illusion because it was based on separation. Separation is the ultimate illusion. You are not now, nor have you ever been, separate from the many versions of your Higher SELF. Feel this divine unity and see it shining through the clearing fog.

~LISA~

"Wait a minute. My dream! I remember my dream. I was standing all alone, but the Sun was shining through the fog and it felt so very good. NO, Lisa, NO! You are just sleep deprived. Don't start believing this crap," said Lisa to herself. However, she could not seem to get quite as angry as before. What was going on here? She needed to get home to her 'normal' life. But, she did not get up or leave. She stayed in her 'homework chair' in her mother's house and continued to read.

~BEVERLY'S JOURNAL~

Mytria's letter continued:

Feel the warmth of the Truth of Unity with ALL THAT IS. Know that you are now at ONE with your divine self. You are the fingers on the hand that is connected to the heart, mind and spirit of the Creator.

I, Mytria, am you on a higher vibration. I am one of your alternate realities, and I welcome your awareness into my world. My true relationship with you is a difficult concept for your third-dimensional mind to understand. Merely listen. I am you, but I am also more than you. However, you are also more than me.

I am not better than you just because I vibrate at a higher frequency. It is just that from my higher perspective I am able to see all of you. On the other hand, you can only see portions of yourself from your dimension. Therefore, I can be of service to you.

From my perspective, I can see you in many third-dimensional realities. I am particularly drawn to the lives in which you served the Goddess, as that was very harmonic with our purpose in this reality. I will be happy to assist you in your communication about the reawakening of the Goddess on your planet.

However, returning to my vision of you, besides seeing your many third and fourth-dimensional lives, I can see the lives in which you chose to incarnate on other planets and on higher vibrations. You have been able to feel close ties to certain planets such as Venus, Arcturus, Antares, Sirius, and here on Alcyone. I can see a fine nervous system of light that is growing each time you open yourself up to communications with these portions of yourself.

There are actually other galactic incarnations beyond what I have mentioned, but you have concentrated on the ones to which you have the strongest attraction and clearest memory. Allow your memory to be awakened as you visualize your light-filled nervous system. Feel yourself moving beyond time and space.

Remember your other realities like you remembered what you ate for breakfast.

Do you remember when you left Arcturus to begin your adventure of incarnation in the lower vibrations? First you went to Venus to prepare for your incarnations on Earth. When you heard 'the call from Gaia,' you came to planet Earth and began your many third-dimensional incarnations.

In your first incarnation, you were a female who eventually became a Priestess on Atlantis. After the fall of Atlantis, you stayed in Faerie in the fourth dimension until your next incarnation in early England. In that reality, you were half Faerie and half human. Write this story, Lisa. It will help you to clear your mind and open your heart.

~LISA~

"Wait, does that say Lisa? That must be a typo," scoffed Lisa. "Mom always had too many typing errors. Except that there aren't that many before now. I am sure I just imagined that." However, Lisa did not go back to check the text. Did she want it to be for her?

~BEVERLY'S JOURNAL~

Mytria's letter continued:

After each life of great spiritual attainment, you were able to raise your vibration enough to incarnate on higher planes of reality. Many times you returned to Venus to rest and relax. From Venus you often returned to Arcturus.

Remember these journeys, as that memory will further reinforce your light plexus. The memories of Venus and Arcturus are the strongest in your mind because they have the greatest love vibration. As you have already remembered, after each of your spiritual lives you were able to take on an alternate reality, which was actually from your past as well as your future.

You will have to just accept that statement because it is very difficult for you to understand at this Earth moment. All of these extraterrestrial realities were created before your Earth lives, as well as created after them. That is all for 'now.' I will be pleased to communicate more. Remember to call to me before you go to sleep and then write your dreams as soon as you awaken.

Mytria

~LISA~

"Remember to remember your dreams," kept swirling in Lisa's mind. But, she pushed it away. Enough of this reading and lying around; maybe it was time to call the police? However, the next post from Mytria caught her eye, so she decided to read just a little bit more.

~BEVERLY'S JOURNAL~

3-11-96

Dear Mytria,

I had a dream last night of a familiar format that I have come to call "Temple Dreams." In these dreams I perceive myself as flying up into a cloudy, etheric area. At first I can only see what looks like fog, but then I seem to alter my course and slowly fly down into another cloudy area, which glistens with a sparkling light.

Gradually, I adapt to a vision in which I am with a group of people. We are sitting under a huge dome that is held with huge pillars. We all sit quietly while we listen to a magnificent being that is much like my childhood cloud friend. However, the cloud being does not always have the same feel to me, so I think that different higher beings speak at different times.

After the cloud being has completed its speech, a being I call my "guide" appears from nowhere and motions for me to follow it. I say "it" because the guide, who always feels like the same being, is also a cloudy presence with glistening light. My guide transports me to an unknown location where I have an experience, which I call "the dream."

~LISA~

"Just a minute here," Lisa said with surprise. "I think I had a dream like that! No, no, Lisa," she said to herself. "Too much of this Journal. I am getting as crazy as my mother. There has been far too much isolation. I really do need to phone the police." But, Lisa did not phone the police. She did not push away the journal, which she had done many times. She wanted to hear about this dream, so she continued reading.

~BEVERLY'S JOURNAL~

In the 'dream' there were three groups that were having some kind of competition. Much to my surprise, I was the leader of one group and, even more shockingly, my ex-husband, David, was the leader of the other group.

We were in an amphitheater and each group was to go around a large circle together within the time period of 28 seconds. A third group had already finished their race, but that is all I remember about that group. For some reason this dream felt important. Dear Mytria, can you assist me to understand what it meant?

Beverly

My dear Beverly,

I am happy to assist you to understand your dream. The 28 seconds reduced to the number 10 in numerology, which further reduced to the number 1. Numerology is a part of your awareness, is it not? The number 1 represents a new beginning.

The three groups are three waves of evolution. The first group did not complete the cycle within the time that they had allotted to them. Therefore, they had to return to their seats, or physical bodies. In other words, they did not finish their race.

Everyone in the remaining two groups was very excited about their opportunity to "win the race," but the older, wiser members of your group knew that beginnings take much patience and calm awareness in order to bring them into full fruition. You also knew that the journey was not ending but instead just beginning.

David, your ex-husband, represented the male portion of your higher dimensional SELF, and you were in the form of myself, Mytria. Just as I, Mytria, am from the Pleiades, David is from the planet Antares and is actually called Jaqual.

The Elders at the front of the amphitheater were from the Federation of Planets. You seem to have forgotten this part of the dream, but as you stood up to take your cycle/race, you remembered that Love is the key to successfully completing the cycle.

Mytria

~LISA~

Now Lisa had had enough. The thought that her father, who she had not seen in ages, was somehow joining a race with her mother, was too much to bear. Besides, what was Antares? She was not ready to phone the police, yet, but when she read that part of the message she started to cry.

Slamming the journal closed did not stop her crying. In fact, she cried harder and louder. She was alone and no one could hear her, so why not finally have a good cry? When she needed a tissue, the only ones she could remember were by her mother's bed. She found her way there, walked to the nightstand to get the tissue, and began to cry almost hysterically.

When she could cry no more, she lay on her mother's bed, just like she had loved to do when she was a child. Even though her mother had been gone for who knows how long, she could still smell her mother's scent when she pulled back the bedspread to climb into the bed. The sobbing calmed, just as it always did when she went to her mother for comfort.

"What happened to us? We had always been so close," Lisa thought as she drifted off into a deep, deep sleep. In fact, it was the best sleep she had had in months.

Just before Lisa awoke from her much needed sleep, she had a dream in which Mytria said to her mother, "Now I will tell you what really happened last evening. You, Beverly, who is a lower frequency of me, Mytria, and David, who is a lower frequency of Jaqual, were at a Federation meeting. You/I and David/Jaqual talked about the ascension process of your planet and how the awakened ones of Earth could assist.

"The first suggestion was to generate excitement in order to jar the sleeping ones into awareness. However, we decided that the excitement would prove to be too much of a distraction from the process of awakening, and we did not have the 'time' to risk that distraction.

"The second race/idea was to have a mass landing of our ships. However, that idea was too soon, as humanity was still too brainwashed that 'ETs were bad.' We then decided that those who had been awake and aware for a portion of their Earth time would be good leaders if they could share their process. In fact, sharing their process would be a good role model for others.

"The third idea was our best idea in which everyone could realize that ascension takes calm patience, unconditional love and great courage. However, there are not enough humans who possess and can maintain 'calm patience, unconditional love and great courage.'

"Finally, we decided that we, the members of your galactic family, would need to bi-locate into the bodies of already incarnated humans who showed some ability to hold the three qualities of patience, love and courage.

"Bi-location means that we are still in our Galactic self and our multidimensional consciousness, but we also share our essence with a human who is willing to accept our presence. Therefore, I bi-located into you, Beverly, and Jaqual bi-located into your husband, David."

Lisa awoke with the message from Mytria in her mind. Before she could return to her skeptical self, she automatically reached for the writing pad and pen that her mother always kept by her bed and wrote.

"The third idea was our best idea in which everyone could realize that ascension takes calm patience, unconditional love and great courage. However, there are not enough humans who possess and can maintain calm patience, unconditional love and great courage.

"Finally, we decided that we, the members of your galactic family, would need to bi-locate into the bodies of already incarnated humans who showed some ability to hold the three qualities of patience, love and courage.

"Bi-location means that we are still in our Galactic self and our multidimensional consciousness, but we also share our essence with a human who is willing to accept our presence. Therefore, I bi-located into you, Beverly, and Jaqual bi-located into your husband, David."

Too groggy to realize what she had done, she fell back asleep and slept until it was dark.

She awoke with a start to find a completely dark house. She reached over to turn on the light and noticed the pad and pen. "Oh," she said. "More weird stuff written by my mother." She did not notice it was in her handwriting, as she urgently needed to go to the bathroom.

She was alone in the middle of the night and felt a bit spooked, so went around the house turning on lights. She then went to the pantry and found some canned soup and an unopened package of crackers. While the soup warmed, she put a cup of water and the crackers on the small kitchen table.

When the soup was ready, she poured it into a bowl and sat in a chair at the same table that had been there her entire life. After she had eaten her soup and crackers, she realized that she had chosen her favorite childhood bowl and cup and had sat on her "side" of the table.

"Why did mom keep all this stuff?" she said out loud. She was just feeling the familiar anger rise within her when she heard, "Because I love you."

"No, NO, that is not my mother's voice I just heard!" cried Lisa. But it sounded like her mother's voice, and Lisa was beginning to realize how much she missed her.

Leaving the dirty dishes on the table, she went back to the homework chair to continue reading. When she read the last three paragraphs she noticed that she had read it before.

"I am not ready to read this now," she said as she found the clicker for the TV and found an old movie to take her away. When the early morning light entered the living room, she awoke. All the lights were on in the house, so she began turning them off.

When she got to her mother's bedroom, she decided to make the bed and saw the notepad next to the light. "Hey, this is what I just read." She did not note it was her handwriting until she finished making the bed and knocked the tablet onto the floor. When she picked it up, she was finally ready to see that it was her writing.

She ran back to the book to see that the message she wrote was exactly the same as the message in the book that was written in 1996. Too shocked to think, she stuffed the tablet in her mother's nightstand drawer.

"Now I am starting to hallucinate. Too much reading of that journal, my body is stiff from sitting in that chair. I need to take a walk!" she exclaimed.

Lisa tried to walk away from the fact that she had written exactly what her mother had written long, long ago. She must have read those paragraphs before, she told herself. "But how could I get every word exactly correct?" she muttered as she began to jog.

By the time she got back home (was she calling it home?) and took a shower, she had forgotten the incident of the "three paragraphs." She finally made some calls to her friend and husband, knowing they would go to voice mail at that time. Then she went to the grocery store to get some decent food. She fixed herself a good dinner and opened up another bottle of wine. Had she been drinking too much lately? She decided NOT to ask herself that question.

When she opened the journal to read while she ate, she conveniently opened to the next chapter, in which she met Jaqual. She knew inside, but had consciously forgotten, that Mytria was her mother and Jaqual was her father. She could not bring her father into the picture yet, or she might completely snap.

Therefore, she unconsciously decided to forget about her parents' higher identity by scoffing at the entire idea of other realities. She was more than busy trying to find out how to get along in just one physical reality and didn't seem to be doing too well at it. Hence, her parents' relationship to Mytria and Jaqual was conveniently forgotten.

III
~THE JOURNAL~
Meeting Jaqual

~BEVERLY'S JOURNAL~

4-20-97

Dear Journal,

Before I continue with my journal, I wish to speak a bit about how this process has changed me so far. As you can see from the dates, I began receiving these messages many years ago. However, I stored them away in the depths of my closet and kept them as a secret, even from myself.

When I began the process of collecting these messages from their various hiding places, something started to shift inside of me. I had to keep these communications away from my husband, who unfortunately I still love, and my daughter, who I will always love. They both have abandoned me, or did I push them away?

As I read these messages it is as if it is the first time I ever saw them. How could I forget something as important as messages from a higher world? Actually the question is how could I forget myself. I see now that these messages are like life's blood to me, yet I stashed them away for the approval of a husband and daughter who both left me for a better life.

Now, I realize how alone I have felt since I made the choice to hide my true SELF in the hopes to hold onto love from another. Perhaps my own inner conflict tainted my love for my family. Something did, as they left. They left me alone with no one and nothing to do. I got the house free and clear from the divorce and enough inheritance from my parents that I do not need to work.

But I did need to work or slowly wither away of loneliness. So I found positions in hospitals, convalescent homes and nursery schools. Maybe they would accept my love, which they did. But they did not return it. It was not appropriate. I was not their family, but a substitute for the ones who had abandoned them.

I went on like this for several years until I finally pulled up these old messages in a desperate attempt to find meaning in my life. I was more than surprised to discover love. It was not personal, conditional love that was based on what I could do for them. No this was transpersonal, unconditional love based on what they could do for me.

As I re-read through the messages from Mytria, I felt such unselfish, sharing love that I felt ashamed. I realized that I had never given that kind of love to anyone. Not to my husband, my daughter or even the very old and very young that I thought I was helping. The reality was that I wanted them to help me.

I was so busy looking outside of myself for love that I did not realize that all along I was receiving wonderful love from deep inside my own self. In fact, as I write these words, I feel the tears rolling down my face, but they are not sad tears. These are tears of joy and thanksgiving that after a lifelong search I am NOT alone.

My sorrow lies in the fact that this inner world was always with me, but I never recognized it. I guess that was because I never recognized myself.

Beverly

~LISA~

As Lisa read her mother's final comment, she too felt tears well up in her eyes. She also realized that it felt better to cry for someone else for a change rather than her own constant self-pity. In fact, Lisa missed her children for the first time, and back in the corner of her heart, she missed her husband.

"Enough of me," she said as she reached for a tissue. "I want to find out more about this Jaqual person who is supposed to be some higher version of my father."

Wiping her eyes, she turned her attention to the Journal.

~BEVERLY'S JOURNAL~

4-28-97

Greetings, Beverly.

I am from Antares. We are in the constellation of Scorpio, serving as the defenders of this quadrant. I, Capt. Jaqual, speak to you from the timeline of my warrior days. The energy fields of our home world in the star system of Scorpio are similar to the energy fields on the planet Pluto in your Star System.

You have heard our call today because it is time that you become conscious of my reality. Your reality has been very different than mine. I am a warrior here, but I have retired from active duty. I recently have entered the Temple where I can focus my attention on my inner life.

My life exists in a different timeline than yours and I resonate in an entirely different area of space. For most of my life, I was too busy battling "the enemy" to deeply look inside. I was a warrior for fifty of your Earth years. That seems like a long time to you, but we Antarians have much longer lives. We usually live about 150 to 200 of your Earth years.

We on Antares are usually fifth-dimensional, but the warriors and the parents resonate to the third dimension when "working" and go home to the fourth dimension. The parents bring their new life down from the higher dimensions to begin their "time in form" in the third dimension.

We function this way so that our children will be strongly rooted in a physical form to be able to procreate and be protectors of our quadrant of space. It is similar to your salmon that leave their natural saltwater to spawn in the fresh water. Antares is a center for multidimensional awakening.

We keep our third-dimensional reality alive and active even though we could all raise our frequency above it. The reason that we do so is because we first colonized this area to assist in protecting those around us, as well as your world, from the Orion Draconians. What the Draconians have mastered with technology we have mastered with our minds.

Since we serve as protectors, at least until the end of your Great Cycle, we have a strong warrior class. The leaders of our societies, as well as most of its citizens, resonate to the fourth and fifth dimension. Almost all of us, male and female, have spent at least 30 years in service as a warrior. I spent 50 years as a warrior, which is common only for the officers. Women are trained right along with men and are totally equal in all military actions.

On the other hand, men are not totally equal in the conception and childcare department. One does not become a parent until after their service as a "protector" has been fulfilled. We warriors use the word "protector" rather than "soldier." We do not fight because we are told to or because we want to gain power and conquest. We fight only to protect our people and our way of life.

Not all people on Antares become parents. In fact, less than 10% actually mate and give birth. However, almost everyone is actively involved in the raising of the young. Persons must go through a major initiation to become parents, much like on Arcturus. However, we do not choose parents by aura color, as they do on Arcturus, but rather by initiation.

The initiation for parenthood takes three years. One must be a master in multidimensional awareness before they can be a parent. This mastery is best described by saying that a master can expand their vibration from the third to the seventh dimension of Oversoul. Also, they are able to open the channel to consciously be aware of all of these dimensions at once.

This expansion of consciousness and awareness is a great feat and the reason why only 10% of our people are parents. In order to become a parent, two harmoniously matched Souls raise their vibration into the Oversoul and invite a spark of life to enter our Antarian world. They then "walk" that spark down through each dimension and "plant" him/her in the female's third-dimensional form.

The Temple that I will soon enter is the one that teaches us to be parents. I feel that since I have taken so many lives that it is my best service now to bring in a new one. Couples usually only have one child. It takes three years to prepare (only 30% of those who enter the initiation complete it) and then another three years to "walk" the Soul down into the third dimension.

Then for three more years, the parents completely dedicate themselves to the raising of the child. At the end of that three-year cycle, the child has become an adult and joins the society. They usually study for about 30 years and then join the military. As you can see, most parents are about sixty years old before they are able to begin the process of preparing for parenthood.

However, since all parents have mastered multidimensional awareness, they usually live to be at least 300 years old. Some live to be 400. The last hundred years of their lives is usually spent in assisting others to become multidimensional. Once one is multidimensional, "death" is just a change of octaves.

There are, of course, others who die in battle, but this gives them a boost to at least the sixth dimension. Their lives are shorter, but their journey into the seventh dimension is easier. In our world, all individuation processes, or individual lives as you would say, originate in the seventh-dimensional Oversoul.

We are asked to leave the Oversoul by our parents when we are "sparks of light." Then we must return to the Oversoul before we can again take another incarnation on Antares or an Arcturian world or Starship. The Arcturians' and Antarians' realities are both multidimensional in nature.

We both focus on assisting people, planets and star systems to embrace their multidimensional essence to ascend back to their Oversoul SELF. Those who find this process of raising their vibration back into the seventh dimension too difficult often incarnate on other planets and star systems. They may also choose a different version of reality for a variety of experience.

Capt. Jaqual

(Note from Beverly:
Almost three months passed before our next communication. I cannot remember why I stayed away. In 1997 I doubted myself and wondered if I was a bit crazy.)

7-1-97

Dear Captain Jaqual,

I am Beverly. I have not connected with you for a while, but I would love to connect with you now. I was feeling you today while I was working out. I heard that you could assist me in being a warrior.

After reading your last message, I realize that you can greatly assist me in my process of becoming multidimensional. I do not think there is any Temple on Earth to teach me those things. Perhaps you could share with me what you are learning in your temple experience.

Beverly

Dearest Beverly,

I can definitely assist you with the mastery of your physical habits and programming. The ability to truly be multidimensional is what allows you to gain mastery of third-dimensional issues and challenges. I can also assist you to rise above your fear.

When one is able to raise their vibration to a dimension above their fear, they have begun their mastery training. That is part of the reason why my people have chosen to be warriors. A warrior must learn to face the fear inside of them. Once that fear is confronted and conquered, then they can raise themselves into their higher vibrational self.

Capt. Jaqual

~LISA~

Jaqual's final words about a warrior facing fear inside himself struck Lisa like a splash of cold water.

Suddenly Lisa realized that all her sadness and anger were actually fear. But, what did she have to be afraid of? Well, start with her husband being with another woman, like her father was with another woman.

Well, that was pretty redundant and very frightening. Then, what about her kids? Would her husband get the kids and she would be alone like her mother? Would she have to desperately write imaginary letters to a man on a different planet in a different star system? Talk about a long distance relationship!

What if her kids abandoned her like she had abandoned her mother? No, that would clearly be the worst scenario. But, had she even spoken to her kids since she "ran away from home"? How could she have been so angry or sad or maybe even scared, to treat her kids in that fashion?

Of course, she came to her senses in the middle of the night so she could not call anyone. What was wrong with her? How could she be so selfish? How could she be so frightened? Maybe this Jaqual could help her out.

~BEVERLY'S JOURNAL~

7-23-97

Dear Jaqual,

I am Beverly, returned to hear more from you. I have felt your call over the last couple of days, but avoided you because I was afraid you would talk about mastering my fear. I have always had a problem with facing my fear. I am ready now to totally release that "problem" and live in my courage.

Beverly

~LISA~

"This is getting spooky," Lisa muttered to herself. "I did not see what mom wrote next as I was too wrapped up in myself. How can this be? How can these weird messages seem like they are addressed to me? Am I hallucinating or something? No, no! I am not going there now. It is just some kind of a coincidence. That is all it is." She whispered as she continued to read the Journal.

~BEVERLY'S JOURNAL~

Dear Beverly,

I am happy to hear that you are now ready to BE the warrior that you have always been. You have been afraid because you were frightened as a very small child and were unable to communicate that fear to anyone or to ask for protection and comfort. That fear has maintained a hold on your subconscious for most of your life.

As you now understand, everything that happened was part of your Divine Plan to awaken to the memory of your Higher SELF. If you had gotten the comfort you needed in your physical world, you may not have gone deep down into your subconscious and high enough into your Higher SELF to find the protection and comfort that you needed.

Now in these closing chapters of your adventure of taking earthly incarnations, you must clear your subconscious of unnecessary fear. We say "unnecessary" because we do not want you to erase all fear. Fear in itself is not your enemy. Fear only becomes your enemy when the messages it has given you remains after fear's purpose has been served.

~LISA~

"Now there was another message right to me." Lisa scoffed. "Maybe I should be a big girl and just listen to what daddy Jaqual has to say."

Was Lisa finally ready to look at herself? No, she avoided that thought and returned to Jaqual's note in the Journal.

~BEVERLY'S JOURNAL~

Fear is a messenger that is telling you to be aware and careful. Without fear you could not survive in the third dimension where there are many dangers. Therefore, when I tell you my story, remember that fear is actually our friend. Fear's purpose is to warn and protect. It is the *memory* and *threat* of fear that is the enemy.

If past fears cannot be released, they become a heavier and heavier burden. Also, if you do not trust that the appropriate warnings will come at the necessary time, then there is fear of the future. *Fear from the past* is the message that is gone and *fear of the future* is the message that has not yet arrived.

When you can live in total trust of and surrender to your Higher SELF, you be able to release all old fears into your higher vibrations where they can be transmuted back to light and love. You will also trust that all your warnings will be timely and lead you in the direction that will always afford you the greatest protection.

We learned these lessons on Antares, and they are the lessons that allowed us to learn how to raise our vibration into our higher dimensional selves. Please remember that I am translating my words into English for you to better understand. Also, I am not of your timeline.

Therefore, as I perceive you, I experience all of your lives in one package, like a book. I can look at any portion out of sequence, or even change the sequence of your life. It is the same manner in which you can perceive my life. This is why you have often felt confusion about the timelines of my Antarian life.

To your perception, I am in all these eras at once, and you can view any timeframe you wish. I am a young Lieutenant (your term) at the same moment that I am an older man. Perhaps as you learn and remember more of *our* Antarian life you will be able to embrace my mode of multidimensional perception. Then you may even be able to remember and understand more Antarian concepts.

~LISA~

"Did Jaqual just say 'our' life meaning that my mother was there with him?" wondered Lisa out loud. "Oh, now I am talking to myself, just like mom used to do." That concept frightened Lisa, as she was finding many ways in which she was like her mother. Should she continue reading like her mother said or just call the police? "Finish reading!" she said, pretending she was following her mother's advice. Actually, she really wanted to know what the journal had to say. The next section was another note from Jaqual, again channeled by her mother.

~Beverly's Journal~

9-25-97

Dear Beverly,

I wish to tell you now about our *Temple of Remembering*. The Temple of Remembering is where we return after our service to community is completed and we are ready to return to the higher dimensions of our world. Before we can enter the Temple we must go through a series of seven doorways with each one resonates to a higher frequency.

There are seven doorways. When we can enter each doorway, we must cross the threshold and walk the hallway before that door. Each series of threshold, hallway and door is of a higher frequency, which emanates the next highest frequency color, vibration and tone.

Each of the doorways represents a "life review" for a different era of our life. In order to pass through each frequency of doorway we are called upon to transmute every lower dimensional experience of that era of our incarnation.

In this manner, we experience an intimate life review through which we can transmute our fearful third-dimensional memories, thoughts, emotions and actions of each successive era of our life into fifth-dimensional unconditional love.

Via the power of our unconditional love, we can transmute back to our true form of Lightbody. If we die in service to our people, we automatically move through all the doorways and onto the highest dimension.

The *first doorway is* **red** and represents our early childhood.
The *second doorway is* **orange** and represents our coming of age.
The *third doorway is* **yellow** and represents our duty as a Spiritual Warrior.
The *fourth doorway is* **green** and represents our time mating and parenting.
The *fifth doorway is* **blue** and represents our transition from parent to leader.
The *sixth doorway is* **indigo** and represents the awakening of our higher perceptions.
The *seventh doorway is* **violet** and represents our transmutations back into Lightbody.

I will now tell you of my journey through the Temple of Remembering. The *first doorway is red* and represents my early childhood. I will tell my story in the NOW, as that is how it lives within my consciousness.

I am standing in front of the Door of the Temple of Remembering. I have always considered myself to be a very large man, even by Antarian standards. It is quite normal for a man to be eight feet tall and many of the women are seven or even eight feet tall, as well.

I am nine and a half feet (according to your earthly measurements) and always stand with my head above most crowds. However, as I stand before the *Doors of Remembering* at *The Temple of Remembering* I feel very small.

There is a series of doorways without doors leading to the actual door. Each of these doorways emanates a different vibration. Therefore, each doorway is a different color and emits a different tone.

I feel a pull on my body as I stand before the first threshold. I have been instructed that as I cross each threshold and stand in the hallway before the next doorway, I will experience different lessons and challenges. These lessons and challenges need to be cleared and balanced before I can proceed to the next threshold.

The first doorway is very close to your color red. As I cross the threshold I am flooded with the memory of my parents. I have not thought of them in many years. I see the brilliant violet eyes of my mother and the deep green of my father's. I feel their dedication to me and know that they studied for many years in order to give me a body.

I perceive my infant self as I am just awakening to my third-dimensional form. Everything is very red and orange and I am hearing the singing of my mother and the laughter of my father. I feel safe and totally surrounded by love. I can still remember the formless world from which I have just emerged. I miss the feeling of being ONE with everyone and everything, but I still feel safe because I am ONE with my parents.

Now my memory moves forward to the time when I am about four. I have been in a hard-shelled body (the word we use for our third-dimensional form because our other forms are far more fluid) and have reached about six feet of height. On Antares we are independent of our parents at three years of age and gain our full adult bodies by the time we are seven years old.

I now live in one of the communal homes with the other children. There are certain adults who run these homes, but we are free to go anywhere in our community and spend time with anyone we please. My mother is an artist and spends much of her time on the fourth and fifth dimension but visits me often. My father comes to see me about once a year. He is a Priest in one of our temples. He assists those who wish to enter the Temple of Remembering.

Suddenly, I feel my first experience of fear, because I am remembering the attack of the Draconians on our small community. I was in the garden of my parents' home visiting with my mother. She loved to visit with me there and was constantly educating me about the many beautiful flowers that grow on our planet. Mother's dear friend, Alicia, had just left the garden to bring us some aboromium tea when we heard a horrible scream coming from the house.

Mother and I raced in to see what was wrong and found Alicia on the floor in a pool of blood. Two huge Draconian reptilian men stood over her. Mother ran to her friend's side and one of the Draconians grabbed her by her hair and pulled her up to meet his eyes. I could not think or plan. I reflexively ran to my mother's aid. I was much smaller than the Draconian warrior, and he laughed as I beat upon him to release my mother.

I will never forget the laughter as the two men observed a boy trying to rescue his mother. Finally, the warrior became tired of this game and used my mother's body to bat me away from him like a small insect.

The other warrior then picked me up and threw me out of the window and into the garden. I will never understand why they did not come out to finish me off. Perhaps they thought I was dead. I'm sure that I must have looked dead. Both of my legs and one of my arms was broken. The left side of my face was bashed in and I was covered with blood. I still have the scars over my left eye. When I finally regained consciousness, everything was quiet and still.

I dragged my body into the house with my one good arm and found my mother dead beside her friend. I can't bear to think what they did to her. It was then that I swore I would be a warrior for as long as it took to seek revenge and find peace. I fear I cannot cross this first threshold of blood red before I release my need for revenge. Only then will I find my inner peace. Perhaps, Beverly, you and I can seek that together.

Capt. Jaqual

(Note from Beverly:
I was so sad and frightened by Jaqual's story that I did not continue our communication. Instead, I went back to speak with Mytria.)

~LISA~

"I do not understand why Mom stopped communicating with Jaqual. I know I should go to sleep, but first I want to know what Mytria has to say," Lisa muttered to herself.

IV
The Journal
~My Return to Mytria~

~BEVERLY'S JOURNAL~

6-15-1999

Dear Mytria,

It is Beverly here. I read Jaqual's story about the death of his parent, and I was so upset that I stopped journaling him. How could I abandon him? Why am I so weak? Please assist me. I know I need more strength and courage. I also realize that in some weird way I do not want to get too close to him.

I must admit that I am afraid to connect with a man who is on a different planet in a different solar system because I have not gotten over my husband leaving me. Please help me, Mytria. I need some strength. I have become so weak that I could not contact any of you in almost two years.

I must admit that they have been a very grim two years. Something snapped in me when I heard Jaqual's story, and I stayed away from all my journaling. I went back to therapy, but I could not put my heart into it. Then I tried some meditation classes, which actually did help.

In fact, I only have the courage to return now because I have been meditating for over an hour. I found that it was best for me to arise as early as possible, before the sun rises. Then I am in my chair, candles burning with soft music meditating as the day begins. The meditation regimen has been going on for maybe eight months now, so I have found the courage to return.

I know that may sound silly to you. Why would I need courage to talk to wonderful beings such as you and Jaqual? You see it is not about you. It is about me. How can I be sure that I am not just crazy, or making you up as I go along? I don't actually think I AM crazy, but I am driving myself crazy with all my doubts and self-judgment.

Mytria, please help me.

Beverly

~LISA~

Just as Beverly doubted her sanity, Lisa doubted hers. How could it be real that she just up and left her husband and children? She knew that she should call her family as soon as they were awake, but she was not sure if she would make that call. Lisa had always seen herself as a very responsible person who always did everything that her husband and children needed.

The house was cleaned, the family was fed, and she always got the kids ready for school, took them there, picked them up and helped them with their homework. She was a much better mom than her mother. She had tried not to think that about her own mother, but her true feelings just slipped out.

I was 5:00 a.m. now, so she would stay awake and keep reading so that she could call the kids at 7:00. She wondered how her husband was doing with getting them to bed and up in time to get ready for school. She had only been gone a few days, but it felt like several lifetimes.

Maybe she should talk to her husband this morning, she thought as she returned to the journal to find Mytria's reply to her mother's cry for help.

~BEVERLY'S JOURNAL~

My dearest Beverly,

Please know that all the challenges of your third-dimensional life are simply glasses that create the projection of the 3D illusion known as physical life. Since you have called for me today, I believe you are ready for me to speak of my home in the Violet Temple of Alycone, Pleiades.

Yes, my dear one, you do deserve and are now a member of that great hierarchy. I have come to remind you of that so you do not become lost in the day-to-day tasks of survival. Also, I do not want you to judge yourself because you feel you are not "good enough."

Your physical plane is coming into a great transformation. I have been sending you inner images of your/our life in the Pleiades, so that you can remember that reality is created by your state of consciousness. I also hear you thinking, "If I create my own life then why did I create a reality where there is only work and struggle?"

My dear Beverly, you have judged yourself your entire life by the yardstick of your outside society. However, you constantly followed the call of your soul. That call did not lead you into focusing your attention on what society deemed as successful. Now, you need to love yourself and love the life that you have created.

See yourself now in the Violet Temple of Alycone. Yes, the first thing you see is yourself flying just above your Pleiadian home. It is small and made of crystal; it is filled with light and surrounded by beautiful trees. You could instantly beam to your home, but you enjoy the act of flying in your fifth-dimensional form.

As you enter your abode, you see that it is filled with beautiful flowers and plants. You have birds that fly throughout your home and another small animal that looks like a dog but walks on its hind legs and has opposing thumbs on its hands. We call them larnacks. They are loyal friends and enjoy domestic duties.

Your larnack is not a servant but a dear friend. He enjoys what he does for you and you love each other greatly. As you go through your day, remember more and more about your abode and the personal life that you enjoy here in the Pleiades. I have focused on your personal life rather than the temple because that is the area of your life there that has the greatest challenges.

You are now finding the line between denial and acceptance. You are discovering how to do the best you can do under the circumstances that you are in and accept the results as being beautiful. In other words, you are learning to live your life from our own point of view rather than from the perspective of your society.

Now Beverly, go about your day and feel me inside of you. Know that one of your true selves is the flowing violet being that you see as me, Mytria. Remember that all your realities are created by your consciousness and that the challenges of your third-dimensional life are simply glasses that create the projections of the illusion known as physical life.

Enjoy your illusions. Soon they will be no more, and you will live in the reality of your true self. There is no time. Therefore, there is no hurry. You must be gentle with yourself. Do not add any more challenges to your life. You have had enough and soon even more will come on their own.

Mytria

~LISA~

"Oh no, not more challenges," said Lisa, as if Mytria was speaking to her. Well, maybe they were all speaking to her. That is, her mother, Mytria and Jaqual. Lisa slammed the journal shut, put it on the nearby table and got up out of the chair. She went into the kitchen, trying to decide whether to have wine, coffee or tea.

Mostly, she just needed to get away from that book, her mother's insane ramblings with unknown beings and, mostly, she needed to get away from the feeling that the people in the journal felt very real and even familiar.

"No, that is not an acceptable thought," she said as she shut the cupboard after getting a new wine glass. Lisa had to admit that she wanted the wine, even though it was still before dawn.

"This is not the time to think about that," she said as she poured the wine. "I am here alone and there is no one to judge me. If I want this wine, I will take it," Lisa loudly declared to herself, as she returned to the journal.

~BEVERLY'S JOURNAL~

7-4-1999

"Welcome again to the Violet Temple," Beverly heard Mytria say into her heart and mind. "We send you love. With our love we can assist you in meeting your daily challenges. We are also guiding you to find your path. The old world is dying now and is to be replaced with a new one. Within this new world there will be many changes that those from the old world will not be able to accept.

"There is an opening of the veil of illusion that will allow those who dare to see many truths that have been hidden. Your planet is one of free will. Therefore these truths could only be hidden because the majority of the society did not want to see them. That majority is diminishing. They are diminishing through old age and they are diminishing through fear.

"Because of their fear they will not allow themselves to see what is coming, so their souls are contacting them. Perhaps with help from their higher self some of the many who still slumber can awaken from illusion. This illusion has created a reality that seems familiar and that familiarity feels safe for them.

"In the midst of the many changes that will escalate logarithmically, these people will cling to the old. However, the old is dying and if they cling to it, they will feel as though they are dying as well. The rules of evolution state that those who are resistant to change are doomed to extinction.

"Many of you, however, are tired of the old and never could embrace it in the first place. It always felt like a lie to you because it was. You are the ones who will now blossom in the new age. You see how your old familiar life is leaving? Be not attached, for attachment retards change.

"You are among those who will openly embrace this change. Those of you who embrace this change shall be the elders in the new reality that is now being created. Now, dear one, allow yourself to revisit your home on the Pleiades.

"Observe yourselves flying over the beautiful green lands. Beneath you are the lovely crystal domes that are peoples' homes. There are many different domes and many different colors. As you fly higher you discover that there is what you would call a neighborhood with a large dome in the center, which is usually white. The colors of the homes change according to the activity of those within them.

"As you fly over our area you see small domes scattered around in the nearby woods, and discover one neighborhood that seems to pull you in. You move towards this area and find that you are instantly standing before your home. You see that it appears to be small from the outside. You do not see a door, but once you desire to enter the dome, a door appears and you walk through.

"Once you have entered your dome, you find that it is much larger than it appears from outside. This is because we are a fifth-dimensional society. Therefore, we are not bound by any constraints of space. You realize as you wander around your beautiful home that anything that you ask for is instantly manifest. Anything that you dream of is there by your side.

"When you settle into your Pleiadian home, you feel a desire to enter the Violet Fire of Transmutation. It is by entering this Violet Fire that you will return to your Pleiadian Lightbody. You hear the chime, the call of the Central Violet Temple, and know that it is your time to enter the flame. You center your heart and your mind on that experience and in a flash, you find yourself standing before the Violet Temple.

"Because we are a fifth-dimensional society, each of us may have a different perception of the same building, of the same home and each of us can also join into others' perception and join into the group's perception. Take a moment and see your personal perception. Yes, now see the group's perception. To the group's perception the Violet Temple appears as a huge amethyst geode with many towers throughout. Again, as you come to the Temple, there appears to be no door until you desire to enter.

"At the moment of that desire, huge golden doors appear that open in a welcoming fashion. As you enter through these doors, you move into the main entryway. Again, take a moment to perceive your personal experience of this main entryway.

"The group experience is that it is a very large building with several pillars and a stairway built of amethyst that leads up, up, up to a tower. There are several hallways that move out in a circular fashion from the central foyer. As you stand there, you see your guide coming down the stairway to greet you to take you to a room by the Violet Temple.

"Take a moment to perceive how you see your guide. Your guide will lead you up the stairway, step by step, slowly, gradually, and rhythmically in preparation to enter the flame. As you reach the top of the stairway, there is a mezzanine with many doors. Your guide takes you to the door that is perfect for your resonance.

"As you enter the door there is an anti-chamber where you are given a robe. Take a long moment and see your robe. What is the color? How does it feel when you touch it? Now shed all that you have worn before and put on this robe. When you are ready, you enter another room where your guide has been awaiting you.

"You sit down opposite your Greeter in preparation for entry into the Violet Flame. Take a long moment now and listen:

What are the words that your Greeter speaks to you?

What is the intention that you hold as you enter this flame?

What do you wish to transmute in your life and in your reality?

"When you are ready, your Greeter opens the door again to yet another mezzanine, except in the very center is a huge Violet Flame. This Flame begins far, far below you and rises far, far above you. See, hear and feel the shades of violet as they vibrate and shimmer. The Flame goes all the way to the sun, to the stars, to the planets, to the galaxy.

"Feel your emotions, center your thoughts and determine your intention. When you are ready now, your Greeter gently touches you on the shoulder. At the count of three, you must jump into the Flame without doubt, without fear.

"Are you ready? Are you ready to let go? Are you ready to take the leap of faith, Beverly?" says Mytria, turning her full attention onto Beverly.

"Yes!" Beverly writes into the Journal. "I AM ready!"

"Then my dear earthly expression," replies Mytria, "I will give you the count of three. One… two… three! Take the leap, take the leap NOW."

~LISA~

Lisa felt herself step into the Violet Flame. No, wait; was that her mother, Beverly, who was making the leap? She could not tell. Her mind was half asleep, yet fully awake to the vision of the Violet Flame that totally surrounded her.

She stepped into the Violet Flame alone, she thought. But she had the feeling that Mytria was with her in her consciousness. Or, was that her mother? And, was there a difference? As the memory of her dense physical body faded from her mind, Lisa realized that her body was in a relatively formless state.

She was aware of a focus of attention, a beam of light that held her individuality within the flame, and the focus seemed to be on her. No, it must be on her mother! NO, the focus, all the focus, was on her. Was it her spirit, her soul, her consciousness? It was certainly not her body.

"My one," she heard the inner voice of Mytria. "The focus is on your essence. Within the flame, your essence is free of any identification other than the intention that you held, as you leapt into the Violet Flame. Once you state your intention, your essence takes a form that best expresses that intention. What do you wish to declare now?"

"What do I declare now?" thought Lisa. She did not know; yes she did know but was afraid to say it. And so she forgot it. She forgot what she wanted to declare. How could she make a declaration when she did not know if she was awake, asleep, herself, her mother or Mytria?

Her world was changing rapidly. All that she had known as a foundation was leaving and changing. Clearly, it was time for her to create a new reality. She was ready. She was ready to let go and fall into the flow. Almost! But something was still stuck. It was stuck deep inside her heart, stuck to her childhood and to her youth.

What could it be? There was a frozen moment in her heart that needed to be healed, but she would have to *open* her heart to accept that healing. She was aware of that fact because she heard Mytria tell her so. How could she hear Mytria, who she believed was just a figment of her mother's imagination?

That brief moment of doubt made her lose her center, her balance, and her faith in her own process. "What kind of trick is this?" she asked as she pushed the Journal away once again. "I must have had too much wine," she said, not noticing that she was so interested in the Journal that she had not even touched the wine.

But she did not see the wine glass because she left the chair and the table with the full wine glass and the Journal that she had carefully placed on the floor. This was just a dream, she told herself as she went to her mother's bedroom.

She pulled off her clothes and got into the bed. When she reached over to turn off the light, she saw that the small drawer on the nightstand had a piece of paper sticking out of it. For some reason she felt possessed to read that piece of paper. As she pulled it out she saw it was her own handwriting.

"The third idea was our best idea because everyone could gradually realize that ascension takes calm patience, unconditional love and great courage. However, there were not enough humans who possessed, and could maintain calm patience, unconditional love, and great courage.

"Therefore, we decided that we, the members of your galactic family, needed to bi-locate into the bodies of already incarnated humans who showed some ability to hold the three qualities of patience, love and courage.

"Bi-location means that we were still in our Galactic self and our multidimensional consciousness, but we also shared our essence with a human who was willing to accept our presence. Therefore, I bi-located into you, Beverly, and Jaqual bi-located into your husband, David."

"Wait," said Lisa as she drifted off to sleep. "Why is Mytria's message in my handwriting?"

Sleep, or a deep trance, overtook her before she had a chance to answer her own question. Perhaps a dream would answer her.

PART II

V
THE JOURNAL
~ACEA~

~LISA~

Lisa awoke suddenly while it was still dark. She had had a dream that she could not remember, but felt strongly that she must read the next segment of the journal. Bruce was soundly asleep, so she slipped out of bed, got the Journal and went into the living room. As she turned on a small lamp in the corner of the living room, she remembered that her mother's face was the last image she'd had before she woke up.

She wondered why she didn't awaken Bruce, who had seemed so eager to read the journal with her. Pushing that thought aside, she read an entry, which was written in her mother's handwriting. Why didn't she type it? She also wondered why this entry had no date. Pushing that thought aside, she began to read the entry.

~BEVERLY'S JOURNAL~

Dear Journal,

While writing and simultaneously reading the story of Mytria and Jaqual, I was told that they are the higher dimensional expressions of my husband,

David, and myself. There, I did it again. I called David my husband. Well, we are not divorced, even though many, including our daughter, Lisa, believe that we are. It may be unfair to let her believe that, but I never said we got divorced, except in her imagination.

Lisa could never understand the arrangement that David and I have. You see, David went back to the Starship. How could I tell my young daughter that her father had to return to active duty in outer space? Therefore, I didn't. I just let her believe that he had left us, which he did. I wanted him to say goodbye to her, but he said he could not lie and he could not tell her the truth. Hence, he could not tell her he was leaving.

He did tell me though. He told me that I would stay here on Earth because I was stronger than him. He said that he was "just a warrior," but I was a multidimensional priestess. I always got so angry with him when he told me that. However, David was incapable of lying and ONLY spoke the truth. Even though I knew those facts to be true, I always had such low self-esteem that I could not believe him.

I still have low self-esteem, which is why I am organizing this journal. I have trouble believing that I am a multidimensional priestess, but have no trouble with believing that I am "not good enough." If I had gotten past that issue, I could have joined him on the Ship when Lisa left the house. But then she got pregnant right away and had two lovely starseeds.

Since Lisa could not believe that she was a special "chip off the ol' block," I guess she could not believe that her children, and her husband, are starseeds. I do not know who I am writing this message to, likely myself, and of course, to Lisa. I don't know if Lisa will ever read it. Still, I need to prepare this message in a manner in which it makes sense to her if she ever does read it.

All right, I must be honest here. I also need to put all this information into some type of, dare I say, third-dimensional, sequential form. This journal began with millions of notes that were scattered around the house from pre-computer days, then put in files somewhere in my computer, post-computer days.

My first, and very arduous task, was to type in all the pre-computer messages, then organize the messages in the computer. I ended up with more pages of information than I care to count, so I started with putting them in order by date. Of course, how can I collect these inter-dimensional messages that came to me from the dimensions beyond time and put them into sequence?

On the other hand, even I who received these messages cannot incorporate this information into my physical life if they are not in some form of logical, 3D sequence. When David was with me, he was the one to receive the messages, while I held down our illusion of being regular people in a regular 3D life.

We were not supposed to have a child. To have a physical child on the physical Earth, I had to release my fifth-dimensional frequency and limit my awareness to the third and fourth dimensions. That was the greatest sacrifice I can remember making in all of my myriad lives.

I would like to say that I made that sacrifice for my baby, or because I wanted a child, or even because my husband wanted a child. Dearest, most beloved Lisa, I know that you will read this journal. I also know what I am about to say will hurt you. However, I cannot live this lie any longer.

First, I did not know that I was pregnant until it was actually too late for an abortion. Second, abortions were illegal then. Third, no one on the Ship would ever terminate a life for any reason. And finally, my confession, I wanted the baby so David would stay with me and not return to the Ship.

Lisa dear, I promise you with my broken heart that when I saw your sweet face I fell deeply in love with you. But, I was never too good at anything human. I could not make or balance money. I could not clean the house or keep a job. I could not make or keep human friends. But, I promise you that I tried with all my inter-dimensional heart to be a good mother.

However, when David left us, I was beyond sorrow. I was so lonely to go home to the Ship, but you came into me on Earth. This was your home, and I needed to be here with you. David would have loved to stay with you, and still comes into your dream life, but he had to return. And I had to stay here with you.

I guess that once I start being honest, I cannot stop. I did resent you sometimes, and I know that you felt that and resented me a LOT. Somewhere during the loss of my husband, and your loss of your father, we took our sorrow out on each other. I realize that you left the house as soon as you could and chose a college that was "too far" to visit me.

I could have visited you more, but I became too tired of being a human and too depressed to return to my multidimensional self. There were many dark years, which I only survived because of my communications from "Home." "Home" is on the Ship, and my 3D home is just a house. Somewhere along the way I forgot my Mission because I forgot my SELF.

It was only because of these writings, which I am now pulling together in a manner that can make some sense to third-dimensional thinking, that I moved beyond my depression. Unfortunately, you were out of the house and mostly out of my life by then. I hear you thinking, "So why didn't you just go back?"

Since I vowed that this message would be 100% the truth, I will tell you it was because I did not want to be a total failure. It appeared that I was a failure with my marriage, with my mothering, with my working and with my housekeeping. I could not return a failure. I had planned and studied for many of what you would call years to have the honor of taking a physical body. I could not/would not return as a total failure.

Once I made that decision, I began to gather my inter-dimensional communications into a sequence of communications that just may be helpful for others. Finally, I had begun to think of others. Since all financial worries were cared for from when we entered our earth body, I did not have to work for money. But, finally, I decided that I wanted to work for a purpose.

During the day I went to hospitals, hospices, soup kitchens, half-way houses, convalescent homes and poverty areas to see if there was anything I could do for someone else. I had spent too much of my life, and all of my life with you, thinking about myself. Finally, I realized that I could help others.

All the abilities that I had kept to myself, I decided to use for the health and welfare of others. By day I worked for others and by night I began gathering all my inter-dimensional messages in the journal that you see before you. If my truth can assist you in any way, I invite you to read it. I guess if you have found this page, you are reading it.

On the other hand, if you throw it across the room, I hope you put it back together and give it to someone who may need it. You may wonder why this message to you, dear Lisa, is this far into the journal. The answer is simple. As I began to go through my experiences in the higher dimensions and on the Ship, I finally gained the courage to be open and honest with the person I love most on this world—you, my dear daughter.

I love you very much, Lisa. I am sorry that love is different in my world. In my world, love and freedom mean the same thing. But you were only raised on Earth, as a human, and needed something that I did not know how to give. By the time I learned to give love, you were gone and wanted nothing to do with me.

Therefore, I will give you freedom. I have learned how to make enough money for my meager needs, so I have been putting all of my "spending money" from the Ship in an account for you and the children. You will find the book for that account in my safe. You also know where I keep my secret papers, which is where you will find the code for the safe.

I was never able to give you the love that you needed, so maybe I can give you the financial freedom to do whatever you want. This account is only for you and your children for as long as you wear an earth vessel. Please note that I did not add Bruce's name to the account. I will let you decide whether or not to do so.

Love,

Mom

~LISA & BRUCE~

When Lisa finished the message, she did not know if she was sad or angry. Perhaps it was a combination of the two, much like her entire life. Fortunately, before she had any emotion at all, she took the two pages out of the journal and folded them neatly into her robe.

Did that mean that her mother was right, and she should *not* trust Bruce? Or, maybe it meant that she had enough wisdom to tell me to hide the note and find out for myself. With the note tucked safely into her pocket, she put down the journal and stood up to go into the kitchen and get some tea. She was so deep in thought that she almost bumped into Bruce.

"Hey," he said as he put his arm around her. "Why did you get up?"

"Oh, I had a weird dream that I cannot even remember and couldn't get back to sleep," she lied. "I thought I would read the Journal a bit, but decided that I needed some tea first."

"Forget the tea, just come back to bed with me," Bruce said lovingly.

"OK," she said reluctantly. She had just started to trust Bruce and now this letter from her mother made her doubt him again. Her mother was not a warm and cozy mom, as even she had admitted, but she was almost always right with her predictions.

She was surprised that she fell right back to sleep and woke several hours later. Bruce was no longer in bed. She instinctively reached for her robe to find that the note from mother was still in place, but was it folded differently? She was just getting out of bed and putting on the robe when Bruce walked in.

"Hi babe, I had to call and make sure the kids got off to school OK. I have kind of taken to this primary parent role."

Why was it that that sentence sent a chill down Lisa's back? Now she doubted him again. It felt much nicer when that doubt was gone. But since it was back, Lisa hid the note while Bruce was in the shower and went to the other bathroom to take a bath.

"Let's walk to the cute restaurant for breakfast. Then we can come back and read more of the Journal. Tomorrow we can go home, as my mother needs to leave, and I must go back to work."

Lisa nodded as if she agreed, but she knew she would not go back with him. She felt guilty that she had been away from her kids for so many days, but she had to figure this whole thing out alone. She would find a reason to stay later.

They had a nice walk and a good meal. When they returned, Bruce went right to the couch and sat down. Lisa sat next to him, but it did not feel the same as it had just the night before. She was deep in thought about her mother's note and almost forgot that Bruce was sitting next to her.

"How could Mom juggle her life on the Ship and still stay attached to this one?" Lisa wondered out loud.

"What do you mean her life on the Ship?" asked Bruce.

"Well, the Jaqual story was all about ships, right?" stammered Lisa, as she got the Journal off the table and handed it to Bruce. "Are you reading or am I?" she said trying to sound calm.

Bruce silently took the book and began to read. The next message was from a group that they had not ever heard of.

~BEVERLY'S JOURNAL~

11-18-98

Greetings from ACEA,

We are: "All Consciousness of Earth's Ascension."

We are the group consciousness of fifth-dimensional Earth. We call ourselves ACEA because the combination of these four letters has the highest resonance. We represent the grounding of fifth-dimensional Unity Consciousness into the matrix of third and fourth-dimensional Earth. We are always in search of another conscious member.

We say "conscious" because EVERYONE on the planet has a fifth-dimensional self and EVERY fifth-dimensional being of Earth is a member of ACEA. ACEA is not a club which one has to join. ACEA is a resonance, translated into a word, which represents the combined consciousness of fifth-dimensional Earth. On the fifth dimension there is no other way.

All consciousness is joined in *conscious* communication at all times, much like you are now becoming joined with your cell phones and other communication devices. Just as you are individuals, we too are individuals. However, we do not need cell phones or any other mechanical devices to commune and communicate with each other.

Let us take you on a journey to the fifth-dimensional Earth. Yes, we feel your confusion because some writings talk about the "forming fifth-dimensional Earth." But, of course, you know that it is the lower dimensions that are formed from the higher ones; not the other way around.

Therefore, the fifth dimension has been in existence since before the existence of the third and fourth dimensions. We are aware that you must continue with your day. We shall return when you are ready to communicate with us further.

Until then,

ACEA

12-2-98

Greetings from ACEA,

Yes, we do exist. We are real. We say this to you because you have not returned to this Journal since our last communication. We are happy to see that you have returned to further communicate with us. Allow us to tell you more about ourselves.

We are representatives of the Brother and Sisterhood of Light with whom you have been connected for many of your decades. We communicate with you, and many others from the higher dimensions, via the inner planes of reality. We are different from "aliens" in that all of us have earth bodies.

We are, however, also "alien" because we all have been able to connect with at least some of our "off world" personas that simultaneously live on the higher dimensions of other planets and starships. We are pleased that you have found *time* to join us again.

We will now take you on a tour of fifth-dimensional Earth. As we have told you before, fifth-dimensional Earth has always existed. Creation travels from the higher dimensions down into the lower. Therefore, if there is a third-dimensional Earth, then there has to be a fifth-dimensional Earth.

Our task is to consciously connect the two worlds. There is a fourth dimension between the third and fifth dimensions which some call the Astral Plane. We, however, lump the Astral Plane with the Physical Plane. When we speak of conscious connection with the two worlds, it is actually three worlds: physical (third dimension), astral (fourth dimension), and the fifth dimension.

We call fifth-dimensional Earth, Gaia, because Gaia is the Soul Name for Earth. The Soul of Earth is fifth-dimensional just as the Souls of all of Her inhabitants. Therefore, whenever we refer to Gaia, we are referring to fifth-dimensional Earth. We think we have all of the introductions taken care of except to remind you that we are a Group Consciousness. This is why we refer to ourselves as "we."

You are automatically a portion of that "we" because you are able to consciously communicate with us. There is no initiation or ritual needed to enter our group. All you have to do is be consciously aware of our presence and interact with us in whichever way you prefer.

If your creative force flows most naturally through writing, then that would be your avenue of expression. Others may communicate with us and ground the force of our fifth-dimensional energy through dance, music, art, etc. Are you ready now for our journey to the fifth dimension?

Actually, we are not going to journey to the fifth dimension. Instead we are going to bring the fifth dimension to you. We will start with your room. As you look around your fifth-dimensional room, see that it is the same but subtly different. Yes, that is a waterfall in the corner, and those are real flowers growing around it.

All of us in the fifth dimension create living space exactly as we wish. We often fill our living space with running water, plants, birds, and animal life. We choose to have music softly enhance the melody of the waterfall. We do not need a bathroom because we don't need to eliminate or bathe in this dimension.

As you turn the corner into the next room, you will see a lovely, clear pond with warm or cool water, depending on your needs. Observe how the waterfall flows into the crystal clear pond. There are also many lovely ferns that grow naturally along the waterfall and the pond.

Just above the pond is a reflective surface. Look into it now and see your fifth-dimensional body. Isn't it lovely? This form is a "Lightbody," which is usually sparkling white and/or golden. Do you see and feel the light emanations flowing from this body?

Your fifth-dimensional body is about the same shape as your earth vessel, except taller. You are also a bit leaner, but it is difficult to tell since your aura is a continuation of your body and expands or contracts according to your activity.

When you are traveling the inner path to the higher worlds your aura is smaller because you are in "inflow" and pulling the light into you. When you are in "outflow" and radiating the light outward from you for healing or creating, which are the same thing in this world, your aura becomes so large that it is difficult to locate your body within the glow of your aura.

We will stop for now. First, concentrate on grounding one small area of the fifth dimension into your body and your life. It is best to choose the area in which you meditate for that will have the highest resonant frequency. Every time you enter your meditation room, practice seeing your fifth-dimensional world. When it becomes natural for that room to appear fifth-dimensional, you can begin to transmute more areas of your life.

We await our next communication with the Joy of Union.

ACEA

~LISA & BRUCE~

"WOW," said Lisa. "I wish I could have those kinds of experiences."

"So do I," said Bruce.

However, even though they were sharing a beautiful experience, just a whisper of doubt in each other was enough to diminish Lisa's feelings of intimacy. Of course, she did not talk about this, as that was more intimate than she could be while holding doubt.

~BEVERLY'S JOURNAL~

12-29-98

Greetings from ACEA,

Dear Beverly,

We see that you have integrated our last messages and are ready for more. Hence, we return within your NOW to instruct how to use the powerful force of your imagination to perceive the fifth-dimensional expression of your reality. Know that this dimension of reality INFINITELY exists within your world, but your 3D thoughts and emotions have taught you NOT to believe your fifth-dimensional imagination.

The first rule to perceive your fifth-dimensional reality is:

"WHAT YOU BELIEVE IN YOUR MIND—YOU LIVE IN YOUR LIFE."

The second rule is:

"LOVE IS THE FORCE OF CREATION."

The third rule is:

"PERCEPTION *IS* CREATION."

Now, let us look again at your fifth-dimensional world.

Close your eyes first and see your fifth-dimensional world with your mind...

Believe in this world...

Love this world...

Open your eyes and again look at your third-dimensional room with your 3D eyes. Simultaneously, look at the fifth-dimensional world with your fifth-dimensional mind. *Believe* in the vision of your multidimensional mind. L*ove* that vision with your high heart.

Do you see again the waterfall? Can you hear it flow into the lovely flower-surrounded pool? The waterfall is made of *waters of light* that radiate fifth-dimensional colors and tones as they fall on the crystal rocks. This pool responds to your thoughts and can be warm or cool, still or churning, depending on what you desire.

The view out of your window, which is directly next to you, is of beautiful redwood trees or the ocean, again depending upon your desire. Your desk and computer is your communication center where you can contact any Starship, star system, or other earthlings.

If you go into a meditative state, you can also connect telepathically. Gradually, the fifth-dimensional world will no longer be a realm to imagine, it will be the place where you/we live. Your transition is gradual so that you can slowly release your thoughts of limitation and feelings of fear.

At first, our fifth-dimensional world will flicker in and out of your awareness. As long as you are able to remain calm and detached from the third and fourth-dimensional dramas around you, you will experience a moment of calm joy. Within that moment, the fifth dimension can appear.

For as long as you can maintain your higher state of consciousness, the lens to your inner eye will allow you to click into the fifth dimension. You will continue what you are doing except that you will do it in a higher dimensional manner. For example, if you are eating and click into the fifth dimension, you will find yourself in a correlate fifth-dimensional location.

This fifth-dimensional location will subtly change your experience. Since there is no need to eat on the fifth dimension, you will instead be nourishing yourself in a fifth-dimensional way. For example, if you are eating with friends or family, instead of putting food into your mouths, you will be able to feel the nourishing experience of sharing Light with loved ones.

If you are alone, you may instead be meditating and/or moving your form in a creative and joyful way. Or you may simply be breathing in the spirit that is within the Light of the fifth-dimensional world. We capitalize the word "light" here because fifth-dimensional Light is very different from third-dimensional light.

Light on the fifth dimension is alive with consciousness and can change forms with your desire or with its function. For example, the waters of Light on the fifth dimension appear to be fluid, which is actually *liquid light*. Liquid Light can take any form to appear as water, land, sky, flowers, animals, humans, etc. These waters of Light bring into your system a form of nourishment, and you can swim "underwater" for as long as you desire.

When beings first come to the fifth dimension, they usually need to "eat" until they can believe that nourishment is free and automatic and that they do not need to hold any intention towards eating. The need to partake of another life form, whether it is animal or plant, is one of the most difficult changes for new arrivals.

"Fear of survival" is a base program that is established for all third-dimensional life forms. If you did not have *fear of survival*, you will actually *fear that you will not survive*, you would not take the necessary precautions to continue your physical existence. This "survival program" is very difficult to override, even when your body is no longer three-dimensional.

Now allow us to tell you how to enter our world. Joy and peace is the state of consciousness that is necessary to access our reality. Much like one has to choose a number to receive a radio station, you must choose a state of consciousness to access our fifth-dimensional reality.

To expand your consciousness enough to enter our world, you need to detach from the fears and dramas of your physical life. Of course, you cannot deny what is happening around you because it is real. What you must do instead is to see the higher dimension of those lower frequency realities.

Just as you have been instructed to see your higher dimensional room, you will begin to see the higher dimensions of every aspect of your personal life and of the world around you. For example, let us look at politics. Allow yourself to see the higher dimensional aspects of that conflict, whether it is bombings, famine, or political unrest. Do you see the peace, unity and love that is being sent down into the third-dimensional darkness?

Whenever there are great numbers of deaths, there will be many beings crossing over into the fourth or fifth dimension. Many people's beliefs are so entrenched in the third dimension that they "believe" they must go through a physical death in order to accept a new reality. Therefore, for them, it is true.

Some people are able to believe that they can experience the higher dimensions without dying, but they believe that they must go through a symbolic death first. Therefore, that is true for them. In the third dimension you have the belief that death is *leaving life*, but to us in the fifth dimension, death is *returning to life*.

Because the consciousness of the masses is quickly shifting, there will be political unrest. As each person changes their personal consciousness they will wish to change the group consciousness, as well. The fifth-dimensional correlate of politics is a harmonious and united group consciousness. Once there is truly a united, group consciousness, an external government is no longer necessary.

As each person embraces Unconditional Love and moves into the fifth dimension, they will have complete rule over their own lower, selfish urges. No external system of rule is necessary when all members of the society can rule themselves. Furthermore, reality is instantly created by your own thoughts and emotions. If you do not wish to share the experiences of those around you, you simply change your mind by calibrating your consciousness to a higher frequency.

Another component of fifth-dimensional manifestation is that "Love Creates." Love yourself, your activity (whether it is paying a bill or meditating), love what you desire and you will manifest it in your reality. Remember, everything you perceive in the third dimension is a product of the illusion that has been created by the group hologram in which you live.

When you change your personal hologram, you will connect with others who also wish to live within that hologram. You will then serve as a model to others who are wishing to change their hologram.

This ends our transmission for today. Please remember to carry us in your awareness and feel our love. If you can remember to keep the fifth dimension alive in your mind, then you will manifest it in your life.

Remember: WHAT IS IN YOUR MIND—IS IN YOUR LIFE.

ACEA

VI
THE JOURNAL
~Keeping the Connection~

~LISA & BRUCE~

After Bruce read this message, they were both strangely quiet. The discomfort that had arisen between them had become very evident and they both felt uncomfortable. They knew that they wanted to talk about their feelings, but were afraid to be the first one to bring it up.

"I guess my mother was a lot deeper than I gave her credit for," Lisa meekly said.

Bruce responded by putting his arm around Lisa and saying, "Our relationship got way off track. I think it will take more than some hot sex to fix it."

Lisa smiled and placed her head on his shoulder. They quietly sat on the couch for quite a while. Then Lisa said, "I would like to read the next message." Bruce silently passed the Journal to Lisa and kissed her softly on the forehead. With a smile on her face, Lisa started reading.

~BEVERLY'S JOURNAL~

1-2-99

We are ACEA, retuned to commune with you again.

Have you been able to see now how your third-dimensional and fifth-dimensional worlds are connected?

Feel the high vibration of your fifth-dimensional reality and pull that consciousness into your third-dimensional world. Good, now see your fifth-dimensional room around you. Can you hear the waterfall and the birds chirping? Do you see the other animals that share your room with you?

They, too, do not need to eat or eliminate and, therefore, do not cause you work or effort. Some of these animals in your fifth-dimensional room do not exist in your physical world. This is also true of some of the flowers and the beautiful colors that they emanate.

As you sit in your fifth-dimensional reality, feel how your shoulders relax and your heart opens. Your breath is slow and easy and you can hear the music of the spheres. Feel the deep love that resonates from our world. Believe that our Love will assist you in manifesting all that you desire.

Now, take this feeling into your day and carry it with you. This expanded self is who you truly are. The portion of you that appears to be limited, separate, or even afraid, is an illusion. It does not exist.

We know that it is difficult for you to comprehend that who you presently see as yourself, is only an illusion and NOT your true SELF. Therefore, allow us to explain how this is true. You see, you—all of you in the lower dimensions—are also here with us in the fifth dimension.

You went down into the physical plane and got scared. It was the fear that made you forget. Fear caused you to forget to believe that you are really fifth-dimensional, and fear caused you to forget to love yourself and love the reason you came to third-dimensional Earth.

You have all waited and prepared for many lives for this wonderful opportunity to be able to consciously raise your consciousness into the fifth dimension—with the ENTIRE PLANET. What an opportunity!

But, you all forgot. Worst of all, fear made you break the connection to your true, fifth-dimensional self. We of ACEA are the "lifeguards" who are throwing life preservers to those who are drowning in their forgetfulness. Grab that line. Keep the connection.

Go now into your daily life and KEEP THE CONNECTION.

In Love,

ACEA

~LISA & BRUCE~

By the time Lisa finished this message, she was crying so hard she could hardly see. She turned to see that Bruce was crying too. Lisa put the journal back on the table and fell into Bruce's now opened arms. Together they cried, then laughed because they were crying, then wiped their tears and cried again.

"Wow," said Bruce as he reached for a tissue on the side table. "This experience is more intimate than sex."

With that simple sentence, Lisa totally forgave Bruce, and told him so.

"Crying is better than sex?" Bruce teased.

"Hey," she said teasingly, "You are the one who said that."

Bruce was very quiet for a long moment then said, "I never want to lose you."

Lisa stood and pulled Bruce back into the bedroom. Much later they returned to the couch, to see Beverly's comment.

~BEVERLY'S JOURNAL~

This message was meant for me. Did ACEA read my mind?

I DID come down to this frequency to merge the third and fifth dimensions.
I DID forget why I came here.
I DID get so very lost
I DID allow my consciousness to drop.

Thank you ACEA, for reminding me about my fifth-dimensional SELF.

Beverly

1-5-99

We are ACEA,

All that you have read about your dimension and your particular space/time quadrant is true, and much more. You see, the final curtain call is about to be made and all the malefic factions that have participated in the third-dimensional experiment want to "get what they can" while the getting is still good.

Soon, they will not be able to stay on the planet unless they can hold the vibration of Unconditional Love. Nothing in their technology and society has prepared them for this energy field. Those of you who have sought to clear yourselves and raise your consciousness have seen the degree of preparation that your physical form has had to undergo.

You have all felt how difficult it is to function with an open heart. You have all experienced how challenging it is to release the armor that has been shielding your heart, and the Atma within your heart, from the dangers of the external world. The many fearful warnings are important because an enlightened person must not hide in denial. However, do not underestimate the power of Love.

This power is greater than any weapon because it allows you to raise your vibration, as well as the vibration of all that you love, above the danger of ANY malefic force. You see, the fifth dimension is not a place. The fifth dimension is a vibration. Anyone who cannot hold the fifth-dimensional vibration will return to the "place" that resonates to his or her personal vibration.

Also, anyone who would do harm to another is not living in the vibration of love, and they will be unable to maintain any experience of the fifth dimension. In order to maintain a connection with your fifth-dimensional reality, you must totally and completely love EVERY aspect of yourself.

Any area of yourself that you do not love, consciously or unconsciously, lowers your vibration. Therefore, your most important assignment is to continue to remember that YOU are a being of love. Then, test that love against fear, and gather all the information that you feel you must, without fear.

Test your ability to know the truth without becoming frightened. We shall all accomplish our Divine Mission as ONE. You see now how total individuality can cause great cruelties. However, total group, or hive mind, can do the same. As with all levels of realities, it is the "in-between" or "balance point," that is the pathway Home.

Remember that time is an illusion. Begin to switch your thinking to the fifth-dimensional "time" of NOW. In other words, begin to allow yourself to transcend time and live in the NOW. In the NOW, there is no hurry because there is no future appointment. There is no fatigue because there has been no past effort.

There is only the NOW in which you are calm, peaceful, and joyous. Take a moment in the NOW to feel calm, feel peace, and feel joy. Within that moment, time does not move forward and the past does not impinge upon your consciousness. While in this state you can *click into* fifth-dimensional consciousness. See the fifth-dimensional world around you and feel how it is different.

Feel your creative force as you choose to LIVE the reality that you are NOW creating.

~LISA & BRUCE~

At this point Lisa became very still. She put the opened Journal on the table in front of them and turned to Bruce. "I do not feel like I am creating any of my reality. Instead, I feel like I have been letting reality create me. I have felt so alone and lonely. Bruce, what happened to us? Didn't we used to be happy?"

Bruce tried to look into Lisa's eyes, but couldn't. Instead, he looked towards the ground and said, "I know you have not been happy, but I could not figure out what to do for you. You were so distant, like you didn't love me anymore."

"Oh Bruce, I do love you. It is myself I don't love. I realize that I have blamed so much on my mother and thought she didn't care about me. But then I have been treating our children just like my mother treated me. She was always distracted, as if I was not enough for her. I think I have done the same thing to our children and to you. Is that why you have been with Carol?"

Bruce was very quiet for a long time. Finally he said, "I guess if we are to create our fifth-dimensional Earth, whatever that means, we have to start with being honest. I swear I was only with her one time, and it was me who stopped it."

Lisa was very quiet. She was surprised that she was not even angry. In fact, she felt almost relieved that she had at least figured out something correctly. Why wasn't she angry or crying?

"Why aren't you angry or crying?" asked Bruce.

Lisa smiled and said, "I was just thinking the same thing. I think maybe because I finally figured out something, that I am almost relieved. Also, if we had been as close as we have been these few days, I don't think you would have been with Carol."

"No," said Bruce. "That is no excuse. My being unhappy is no reason to be unfaithful. I was being cowardly. Instead of confronting you, I took the coward's way of thinking you didn't still love me. Worse yet, I acted as though I did not love you. But I do love you. I DO!" he said as he grabbed Lisa and held her very close to him. They both began to cry, then that made them both laugh. Simultaneously, their eyes fell on the next sentence in the book.

~BEVERLY'S JOURNAL~

CALM ~ PEACE ~ JOY ~ LOVE.
Feel the power of these words and embed them in your consciousness.

Calm—see a perfectly still pond before you with the sun rising from behind it. This pond is the vision of the Calm that you can feel.

Peace—feels like a forest morning with a flower filled meadow glistening through the trees. This is the Peace that you can feel.

Joy—is the feeling of your inner child laughing at the many new discoveries of life. This child is running across a beautiful field with a small animal following and birds leading the way. This is the Joy that you can feel.

Love—feels like a warm blanket that is wrapped tightly around you while you are held in the arms of a loved one. This is the Love that you can feel.

YOU are the reality that you create!

Good-bye for now. We will return upon your call.

ACEA

~LISA & BRUCE~

"Do you think we can make this work?" asked Lisa.

"If we can create a new reality, maybe we can create a happy marriage," Bruce answered.

The next day Lisa awoke while it was still dark and quietly slipped out of bed. Something was bothering her, and she could not figure out what it was. She did know that this issue was not about Bruce. It was about her. Now that the secret about Bruce was out, apologized for and forgiven, why was she still so angry?

Now that she could see the "real mother" that she always wanted to know, why was she so angry? Then she thought about her children. Since she had forgiven her mother, she woke up realizing that she was being a very bad mother herself. She had abandoned her kids much more than her mother had ever abandoned her.

She had to see the children! She had to go home and see her children. No more handing her parenting off to her husband or her husband's mother. She had to be the mother—right NOW—today. She had to drive home and see her children, but what about her mother? What if she came home and no one was there?

Maybe Bruce could stay here for the weekend, then she could come back when his mother could be with the kids. The fact, she suddenly realized, was what she wanted to see the children alone. She *needed* to be alone with her kids. She needed to hold them, kiss them and love them in a way she had not done in far too long.

"We need to go back today, as my mom needs to leave tomorrow," said Bruce who was quietly walking up behind her. When he saw the look on Lisa's face, he said, "What is wrong? Are you alright?"

Then the tears started and Lisa could not contain them. She wanted Bruce to know that it was not about him, so she stood up, walked over to him, put her arms around him and sobbed into his chest. Bruce stood totally still and held her while she cried.

"It's about the kids, isn't it?" whispered Bruce.

Lisa pulled back and looked into Bruce's face and said, "You are a starseed. How did you know that?"

"Now that my guilt is gone, I no longer need to think that you are only upset about me. Also, I am sure it is difficult for you to blame your mother any longer after she has been so honest and vulnerable with you."

"OK," smiled Lisa. "I think I liked you better when you were just a human."

"Seriously," said Bruce, not allowing Lisa to push him away, AGAIN. "Why are you crying?"

Lisa took a moment to compose herself as she was not sure of the answer, that is, the complete answer. He had been so honest with her that he deserved the truth. Lisa began, "I spent so much of my life judging my mother for abandoning my needs, and now I have completely abandoned my own children. I know that is not all that is bothering me, but I don't think I can get to the rest until I make amends with my children. I need to go back and see them."

"Great," said Bruce. "Let's go."

"No, Bruce, I need to see them alone. I also need you to stay here in case Mom comes home. You can Skype me and read me the next parts of the journal when the children go to bed. I know that sounds really crazy, but I need the four hours alone driving to think. I will get them off to school on Monday, and wait till your mother arrives."

"Did you notice that you just totally left me out—again? What I did with Carol was not OK, but I was so lonely. You were never 'with' me. You were just 'near' to me."

"Yes, I understand that now, and I am not still angry at you about what happened. But, I need to have some time alone with the kids, and I cannot abandon my mother, either. I need you to be here in case she comes back. She will be so happy I am with the kids and you are here. You know how much she always loved you."

"Yes, I do know. I also know that that made you jealous," mused Bruce.

"Yes, yes," said Lisa. "It is time for me to take a long look at myself. I need your help. Your mom will be back on Monday, and I will return to you. Please, let me do this."

"Will you go and Skype and read the journal with me? I can just read and you can listen. Then I can also say good night to the kids."

"Yes," said Lisa trying to suppress her jealousy. "That is a good idea. We will walk to the restaurant, like the lovers we have become, and then I will leave. OK?"

"What if I look ahead in the journal while you are gone?" Bruce teased.

Lisa gave Bruce a soft, loving kiss and went to the bathroom to take a shower.

Bruce stood right where he was for what seemed like a very long time. Something was happening to him. The Journal that had so changed Lisa had also changed him. The reality was, he really wanted to be alone, too. Who was this new person that he felt inside of himself? When he went back to the bedroom to put on his clothes, he saw what looked like a page from the journal.

Lisa had placed that page on the bed, with a sticky note saying, "We can talk about this at the restaurant." He saw that the page had been folded, as if Lisa had kept it from him. When he read the note about Beverly's bank account and the money she had left Lisa and the kids, he knew why. He also knew that he had gained Lisa's trust, but he was not sure that he really deserved it.

When Lisa came out from the bathroom wrapped in the robe that had held that note all along, Bruce said, "Can I quit that job I hate now?"

Lisa ran to him and threw her arms around his neck. "I am so sorry I hid that from you. Can you forgive me?"

"Always!" whispered Bruce.

Much later while walking to the restaurant Lisa said, "I did ignore you. But I was also ignoring myself."

"Me, too," whispered Bruce, shaking his head.

Lisa got up before dawn, put on her clothes, kissed Bruce on the forehead and left for their home. Bruce acted like he was half asleep, but he had been awake for hours. He felt like there was something in the Journal that he needed to read, to help get his bearings.

He couldn't wait till tonight, and he could read again with Lisa. He put on some sweats and t-shirt, grabbed some instant coffee and grabbed the Journal. When he went to the next article he found it was another message from ASCA.

~BEVERLY'S JOURNAL~

1-27-99

We are ACEA, here to tell you more about the forces that oppose you. These forces are the ones who make you feel like you are "bad" if you are unable to keep your commitment to the old structures of mundane physical life. Do not forget that there is another commitment that you all have sworn to keep. That commitment is the one that you made to your Higher Self before you entered your physical form.

You made the pledge that you would not forget who you truly are. You promised that you would remember your true multidimensional self, while you were still wearing your third-dimensional body. This was, indeed, a huge commitment and all of the responsibilities of your third-dimensional life often seemed to be standing in the way of fulfilling your prior promise.

Now you are keeping your first pledge to remember your true Self. However, in doing so, you are having a difficult time re-organizing your life so that your physical responsibilities can be taken care of without being in the way of your first commitment. It may feel as though there are forces beyond your control stopping you from gaining enough clarity to move forward.

However, once you keep your first commitment, which is to remember that you are a multidimensional being who has come to the third dimension to learn and serve, you will automatically take more responsibility for the life *you* are creating.

From your third-dimensional consciousness, it is difficult to take responsibility for ALL of the life that you have created because there is little validation in your external life that you really are multidimensional. Consequently, it is much easier to believe that you are "just third-dimensional."

We say to you NOW that you must learn to totally trust your own inner guidance when it reminds you that you are multidimensional. We realize what we ask is difficult, as we realize that your world has taught to "fit in" rather than "seek the truth." It is a hard task to go inside to find your SELF in a world where the inhabitants are trained to follow others.

However, when you begin your process by believing that you ARE a multidimensional being and that you ARE creating your life, it makes it easier to release your fear. If you believe that someone or something else has created your life and you must follow "them," it is almost impossible to release your fear.

We know that if you believe that you are the victim to others, you will not feel in control of your own life. That is a VERY frightening situation. The secret is to release judgment. Release judgment of others and release judgment of yourself. If you think that the problem is your "fault," you will also feel guilty and ashamed.

If, instead, you take responsibility for the situation, you will feel empowered. Furthermore, once you no longer judge yourself, you will no longer need to judge others. Once you believe that you are creating your life, then, according to the first rule of manifestation, you ARE creating your own life!

You, and your Soul, are choosing your problems to create situations, which will allow your hidden fears to be brought to the surface of your consciousness and released. Fear must be expunged from your consciousness in order for you to keep your First Commitment.

When each of you can remember that you are a multidimensional being who is visiting the third dimension to complete your destiny, you can face each situation without falling into the grip of fear. Free from fear, you will be able to release each "problem" and move on to the next phase of your initiation.

Yes, there are many phases, but you will learn to face each step of your process within the ever-present NOW. Yes, there truly are outside forces that wish to interfere with your progress. We know that most of you are not aware of your power and cannot understand how you could be a threat to anyone. But, the truth is that you are.

You are not a threat now, but your future reality can be. You constitute the initial groups who have introduced the concept of multidimensional awareness. This concept will free the masses greatly from the shackles of their forgetfulness.

You have established a conscious connection with your higher dimensional selves and with other beings that inhabit the higher dimensions. Once the majority of humanity can do that, they will see the world as you do. Then the forces that are now in power will have no influence upon the masses. What good is it to rule when there is no one to rule over?

In Unconditional Love,

ACEA

~LISA & BRUCE~

Bruce could not believe what he had just read. Even though the message was from 1-27-99, it was exactly what Bruce needed to hear. He had acted as though quitting his job was a joke, but the truth was that his mind-numbing job was driving him crazy.

He wondered if he should just let well enough alone, or tell Lisa that the boredom of his job was the main reason for his cheating. NO, he decided, she was OK with it for now, so it was best to just leave it alone. But he had to admit to himself that if he did not get more challenge in his career life, that he would seek it in a woman's bed. Absolutely, he should not tell that to Lisa. But, she did say to quit the job he hated.

"Enough thinking," said Bruce to himself. "I need to take a run. This is actually a really nice neighborhood, and this area seems that it might offer better opportunities. "I will take some money for coffee and a paper after my run, to see what the job market is like here."

That night, Bruce Skyped the kids good night. Lisa put them each in bed and brought to the computer into their beds so Bruce could say good night to each of them. She then took the computer into the den so that she could talk to him alone.

Lisa had so much to say about her drive and her day with the kids, and Bruce told Lisa that he had got a local newspaper to check out work in that area. They laughed, talked and made plans like the best friends they were finally becoming.

After Bruce read Lisa the entry he had read alone, and they laughed at how it was spot on, they realized that they really miss sleeping together.

"It is not even about the sex, it is about the intimacy. I means, yes, the sex is wonderful, but I am surprised to realize how much I love being your friend," admitted Bruce.

Lisa laughed, and cried, and told him how much she agreed. Finally, they threw each other kisses, shut down the computer and went to their separate beds. The next morning they both woke up alone, but with the same memory of being on a huge plane. Actually, it was too big for a plane. Was it a Starship?

Late Monday afternoon, when Lisa finally returned, they talked, laughed and went on an actual date. "How romantic is this?" said Lisa as she kissed him before they entered the fancy restaurant. They ignored the Journal again that night. They were beginning to find their own life, and were less interested in Lisa's mother.

That night they dreamed again about being on the plane/ship. Only this dream included Beverly, or someone that looked like Beverly. The next morning, they decided to return to the Journal in search of more answers. They opened the Journal to the next page, which began with another message from Beverly.

~BEVERLY'S JOURNAL~

Dear Journal,

I do understand what is happening with me. I saw Lisa and Bruce on the Ship last night. It was so wonderful to see them. I am pretty sure that they never remember when we meet here, but I do so love it. Maybe what I love best is the person that I am on the Ship. Why do I allow my consciousness to drop so when I am in the physical world?

1-30-99

Dear Beverly,

I AM Kepier. I know you may not understand this yet, but I am a fifth-dimensional component of your Multidimensional SELF. Everyone on the third dimension has fifth-dimensional expressions of self within our group vibration of ACEA. Collectively, as All Consciousness of Earth's Ascension, we represent the beacon on which all of our third-dimensional expressions of self can set their focus.

If each of you can find your own fifth-dimensional self, your own stream of consciousness that feeds into the great river of ACEA, it will be easier for you to create a life that will remain intact through the narrows and into the higher worlds.

The Unity Consciousness of the fifth dimension is difficult to understand from the third dimension. Our group consciousness does NOT mean loss of individuality. Instead, it means that there is a group that you can completely trust because you know everything about each other.

We understand that this form of unity consciousness is a unique concept in the physical world where each person must learn to protect him or herself in order to survive. It is that "protection," which is indeed based on physical dangers, that creates so much of the fear in your dimension. If each of you can connect with your own fifth-dimensional self, as well as the group vibration of ACEA, you will find great protection and comfort.

From our broader perspective of the fifth dimension, we can perceive possible problems and dangers that are still invisible to you. We are similar to the ranger in the towers on the highest mountain peaks who can view the entire forest. We can warn you if there are any potential "fires." All you have to do is tune into our frequency so that you can hear us.

If each of you can find the portion of your Self that resonates to the fifth dimension, that resonance will create a vibrational bridge which each of you can use to connect with the frequency of ACEA. However, first you must create a third-dimensional life clear enough of fear that you can attune to us and hear our directives.

How do you create a reality that is clear enough of fear to allow you to connect with the frequency of the fifth dimension? Meditating, being in nature, writing, and other creative actions are important in assisting you to raise your consciousness enough to communicate with the fifth dimension.

Doing the "work" that is in resonance with your Soul's purpose is also important, because it will give you the JOY that will expand your consciousness and make it easier to merge with your fifth-dimensional self.

Once you create this pathway, how do you stay on it? LOVE—Unconditional Love! Therefore, it is vital that you allow an outer reality to unfold before you that is of the purest vibration of Unconditional Love. That means that you must continuously commune with your inner reality to gain the wisdom and strength to stay focused on your pre-birth commitment.

Your struggle with the third-dimensional world comes, not just from your circumstances, but also from your fear. Once there is no fear, or at least much less, you will no longer need to create a wall of protection. Instead, you can allow love to guide you through the narrows of life.

You will then be able to identify fear as it enters your consciousness because it will feel "different" instead of "normal." Once you can identify your fear, you can release it to the Unconditional Love that surrounds you on your pathway Home.

Those of you who have chosen to create this "pathway," have allowed a procedure to take place in your bodies that will initiate a gradual rise in the vibratory rate of your cerebral spinal fluid. Your new, higher vibratory rate will facilitate an activation of your Lightbody.

Do not fear or judge the process that will follow. Keep your mind open and your heart clear. Fear and doubt will blur your perception and hinder the process. Remember that you are creating your reality. If you believe that something is impossible, then it is. Allow your mind to be completely open and free of all expectation.

Allow yourself to walk upon the virgin soil of the Great Unknown. Goodbye for now. Know, of course, that we are in constant communication. Feel the Unconditional Love that we send you from the fifth dimension. Feel this love like a homing beam that will guide you to us, ACEA.

From within ACEA,

I AM Kepier

~LISA & BRUCE~

"Mom has a Higher SELF named Kepier?" Lisa and Bruce said together. Then they both laughed and went to get a glass of wine. Halfway there Lisa said, "You know, honey, I think I will just get tea. I realized since I came down here just how much I had been drinking."

"Cool, me too," said Bruce, sending a blessing up to Kepier. Lisa had definitely been drinking too much. That was before they began to read the Journal. As they took their tea back to the living room, they talked about how much the Journal had changed them. They hoped they could find out more about what was happening to Beverly from Kepier.

With tea in hand, they returned to the journal and turned the page. They were happy to see that the next section was about Kepier. They also saw that it was the first entry Beverly had written in almost two years.

"Why do you think she stopped writing in her journal for so long? What was going on with her?" asked Bruce.

"I don't know," said Lisa, with a guilty look on her face. "Mom and I were not talking at all then."

VII
THE JOURNAL
~Meeting SELF~

~BEVERLY'S JOURNAL~

12-23-01

Dear Journal,

I have been hearing a message just inside my mind, or is it my heart? I am asking you now to assist me in recovering this message. I have been communicating with an ascended being that has told me much of his/her process, which is a great deal like mine. We seem like very different people, but our process is very similar.

It has been wonderful for me to be able to talk without any editing of my presentation so that I don't confuse or frighten the listener. I know that I need to do more of that in order to close the gap between the "me" who writes this and the "ME" to whom I write. I was told that I have been communicating with the Arcturian Group Mind.

I am ready to be my full multidimensional expression of SELF. I am ready to close the gap between who I call myself and who is calling me. Please assist me now to better understand this process.

Beverly

Our dearest Beverly,

We, the Arcturian Group Mind, are here to answer your question. You have already closed that gap; it is just a matter of re-calibrating your perceptions to be able to consciously experience ALL the frequencies of reality beyond the third/fourth dimensions.

We know that you miss the reality that you experienced on our Ship. Most of all, we know that you miss BEING the person that you were when you were with us. Therefore, we will assist you to regain your memory.

The Arcturians

Oh, dear Arcturians,

Once you identified yourselves I instantly remembered you. But how can I remember you on the Ship when I cannot remember me on the Ship?

Beverly

Be patient, dear Beverly, and we will assist you to remember that higher dimensional expression of your true, multidimensional self. Go to sleep tonight and contact us in the morning.

The Arcturians

12-24-01

Dear Arcturians,

I woke up tired again. It seems as if the more I sleep, the more tired I am. Is it becoming a habit to sleep so much, or is the habit about being in the fourth dimension and beyond? I like my life, I think. It is just that it is changing so fast, or is it not changing fast enough?

I have so many expectations about what will happen, which is likely a place to hide my fear. I feel I do NOT need drama and challenges to learn any longer, and I think that there are many others who no longer need the harshness of third-dimensional challenges. Nor do we need a catastrophic event to get our attention.

I know we came to Earth to help with a peaceful transition into the fifth dimension, and I am holding that intention. But, there are many who are still asleep, and they may need some good old-fashioned drama to make them take a long look at themselves. On the other hand, there are many people who have been looking at themselves for decades.

In fact, many of them are now seeing the faint image of their fifth-dimensional "Lightbody." That is the reality that I want to create. I want to create the reality where people wake up like blooming flowers—one petal at a time. We don't need to question if it is our time to awaken, for if we are awakening; it is. If we have not awakened, then it is not our time, but it will come soon.

I am getting better at releasing fear and living in the Flow of the ONE. That is, I am ready when I am not too tired, hungry, sick, busy, stressed out or driving in traffic—oh yes, or worrying about my family that I never see.

Then, I get worried and, finally, I realize that all I can do is relax into the process, as there is nothing I can do. I do know that a major part of my process is that I need to gain a better connection between myself here on Earth, as well as with my higher dimensional self on the Ship.

Dear Arcturians, what am I to do to have a conscious experience of the "me" on a Starship? Do I want it too much?

Beverly

~LISA & BRUCE~

"Well," said Bruce. "It appears she was doing something over those two years. She seems to be, I don't know, more conscious. Can I say that?"

"Yes," replied Lisa. "I have to admit that I feel even worse. Here I am judging my mother and not even talking to her while she seemed to be doing some really important work."

Bruce decided to just give Lisa a brief hug, as talking about her relationship with her mother seldom went well. They were both so surprised by the next message that they decided that it would be best if Bruce read it.

~BEVERLY'S JOURNAL~

1-1-02

Dear Journal, and if I can expand my frequency enough, Dear Arcturians,

Here it is, the first day of a new year, and I am totally alone talking to you. I am talking to you because you, dear journal that is actually my portal to the Arcturians, are the only one with whom I can be completely honest.

David, my Divine Complement, is gone to "who knows where," and Lisa, my daughter for whom I stayed on Earth, hates me. I know I was not a very good mother. I had never been around human children. And even though David and I have very little human DNA, our daughter seems to be totally human, with a tiny bit of Pleiadian DNA.

Enough of my self-pity, I must admit that I was never a very good human. David, and I both entered our human earth vessels just after WWII. We came in as babies because the adults were far too wounded.

However, the damage of WWII was not enough. The humans kept on testing nuclear bombs on the body and IN the body of beloved Gaia. Nowhere was safe. They blew up small islands in the ocean, deep underground caverns and vast areas in the desert.

Why did they *not* consider that that energy would go into the Earth and into the atmosphere? However, things were worse than we thought. The "Power Over

Others," Draconians in human clothing, had gone underground—literally—where they continued to rule via darkness.

We, the Galactics who have answered Gaia's call for help by wearing a human form, call these "Power Over Others" groups the "P.O.O." We use this short cut, as we do not want to create a thought form with the essence of their very name.

If the humans knew how dangerous it was after the war AND well into 2012, they would more fully realize how much better it has become. By "better" I mean that the energy fields and floating thought forms are of an increasingly higher frequency.

These higher frequency energy fields are why I am documenting my personal experiences. It was one thing to be able to talk to Galactics, but another to actually document our experiences.

They, the P.O.O., knew that we, the Galactics, were here and we knew that they were here. We had an unwritten agreement. "Power Over Others Realities" and "Power Within Realities" had flowed side-by-side for eons beyond eons. Furthermore, our silent battle was being played by all life on Earth.

The more powerful plants overtook the weaker and the more powerful animals fed on the less powerful. And then there was humanity. The plants, the animals, even the elementals, had a Unity

Consciousness. Although they all fed on each other, they realized that it was all for the greater good.

As the humans evolved enough to be the "head of the food chain," the unity consciousness of the greater good was increasingly replaced with the individual consciousness of competition and domination. The "Garden of Eden" closed and the plants and many of the animals became the *prey* for the human *predator.*

Within the fifth-dimensional "garden" humanity could commune with all life, and all life communed with humanity. But as the Power Over Others polarity of Gaia's world became dominant over the Power Within realities/civilizations, Earth reality slipped out of the fifth-dimensional "garden" and into the third-dimensional matrix.

In fact, this third-dimensional matrix had to be created at the time of the fall of Atlantis, so that life could continue on the body of Gaia. However, Gaia's resonance had fallen from the fifth dimension into the third.

Hence, Gaia's multidimensional matrix, which is the hologram through which energy can live in the illusion of physical form, had to add a low frequency, third-dimensional matrix. Gaia's Multidimensional Planetary SELF survived, but most of her inhabitants became lost in the low frequency patterns of the third dimension.

Finally, after untold eras of darkness, with sprinkles of "peak societies," there are energy fields that are strong enough to create a majority of Power Within, Golden Age, Realities. That is why we, the Galactic volunteers to Earth, are wearing earth vessels within this NOW.

However, I have worn this earth vessel for over six decades and have spent most of that "time" living within the myriad flows of dark and damaging energy fields. The humans all had a lower frequency of consciousness, and many of them were even trapped in fear.

Therefore, the P.O.O. had been able to keep Earth to themselves. They treated Gaia and Her life forms like slaves. But *finally* the tide has turned. Gaia's planet and many of her humans are moving into the flow of the myriad higher dimensional energy fields and thought forms.

For eons, the fear on Earth replicated itself over and over again. This occurred because the frightened humans created many of the thought forms. Fortunately, a small minority of other humans was able to reach and maintain high enough states of consciousness that they could perceive higher dimensional light-streams.

Because these humans could perceive these higher dimensional "light-streams" while in higher states of consciousness, they could serve as portals to pull these energies into their physical forms and forward them down into the Core of Gaia.

It was primarily because of the humans who dedicated their lives to "feeding the Mother" that Gaia was able to remain on Her axis and survive the onslaught of fear, anger, sorrow and greed that continued for millennia.

Because we Galactics wearing earth vessels are telepathic, clairvoyant and clairsentient, we KNOW Gaia as a living entity. We also can *feel* Her planetary sentience because we all had to pass through a very small portal from our fifth-dimensional self and into our present earth vessel.

Of course, all of humanity makes that same journey into an earth vessel, but whereas we can remember that event, most humans have forgotten it. We, the ones who can remember, are NOW here to prepare for the next "event" of our personal and planetary return to our true multidimensional realities.

Unfortunately, many of the hybrids (Galactics wearing human garb) such as David and myself have lost many of our innate abilities since we entered our 3D earth vessels. I remember that when I, my Galactic Self, realized that I had entered a vessel in the "time" of 1946, I was very angry.

When my human self was young, I could still remember my *real world* in the higher dimensions, but my Galactic self knew that Earth would be going through many years of great darkness.

My human child body could not understand why she was so frightened. Something was coming, but she did not know what. She often said to her invisible SELF, "If there is another world war, kill me first." These were actual sentences that she knew not to tell another human, but lived forever in her growing fear and depression.

Fortunately, I did remember many other lives in which I tried to gain a higher state of consciousness and used it in a loving manner. However, as much as I searched, I did not see any realities in which I had actually fulfilled my mission.

Yes, because I was Pleiadian I primarily cared about art, beauty, plants, animals, unity and love. However, those were qualities that were NOT abundant in the reality I had chosen to "grow up" in. By the time I met David, I had entered my return path, but had no idea how difficult it would be.

The 70's were fun and alive and hopeful. However, as the 80s came in, it was clear that we were NOT on the Pleiades. Fortunately, it was around that time that I finally met up with David, my Divine Complement.

We instantly recognized each other and were together from then on. That is, we were together until he was called back to the Ship. For many years I could not leave at night to visit him on the Ship, as I had a young daughter that I had to raise on my own.

Does that sound angry? Yes, well, I was VERY angry, sad, lonely, depressed and terrified. Here I had this human child who always loved her father more than me, and her father had to leave on some kind of secret mission.

I was so devastated by his leaving that I could hardly take care of myself, much less a pre-adolescent daughter. Did I mention that my daughter always blamed me for her father leaving us? OK, I am being the victim again.

I know now that she did not *just* miss him. She missed US. When David left, a great deal of my higher essence left. My human shell was there, but my essence was not. Because of my own disassociation from my SELF, I had to repeatedly remind myself to take care of my daughter.

So, I did take care of her needs. But, I did not take care of HER. Yes, I understand why she hates me, and yes, she does hate me. I am not exaggerating. I feel how she feels even more than she does. Humans have the ability to hide their thoughts and emotions from their conscious mind, but Pleiadians do *not* have that choice.

We Pleiadians developed a reality built on unconditional love, forgiveness and acceptance. Therefore, we do not judge others or ourselves. We

ARE in the NOW flowing through our fifth-dimensional reality in unity and peace.

However, we left our children, humans, untended too long. We initiated their reality then left before the humans were mature enough to rule themselves, much less rule others. In fact, we "left the door open" and the Draconians came in.

But NOW it is changing. I can feel, see and hear the streams of higher dimensional consciousness flowing through the dark sea of the remaining fear and "Power Over Others." We, the Galactic volunteers who took earth vessels to assist Gaia, are entering a possible reality of immense transition towards the light.

So, I STAY. I stay here on Earth, in this body, even though I have lost or pushed away my loved ones. I stay here, not to be with David, because he is gone. I stay here, not to care for Lisa, as now she can take care of herself.

I stay here for Gaia. I do not know how much help I can be while wearing this form, but I do know that I volunteered to do my best. I say this now, after I have lost the two people that were my reason for staying, so that I can remember that I CAME TO HELP GAIA!

Therefore, I close this message saying, crying, shouting and whispering:

Let It BEGIN!!

"But, what is beginning," I ask myself.

"Whatever YOU create," I hear my Pleiadian self-whisper into my human heart.

~LISA & BRUCE~

Bruce became so enthralled in Beverly's message that he forgot about how it may affect Lisa. That is until he finished reading and turned to her to see that she was as white as a ghost with tears streaming down her face. He reached over to put his arm around her to comfort her, but she angrily pushed it away.

"What is wrong?" he asked in a confused manner.

"Oh, now you care!" she said as she pushed him away from her.

"What—what do you mean? I don't understand," Bruce stammered.

"Yes," snapped Lisa, "you don't understand. You NEVER understood. You were so busy with your life, your job and your decisions. Even now, you didn't think one time to look at me or comfort me when my mother confessed that she never loved me."

"That is not what she was saying...." At this point Lisa got up and tried to leave the room.

Bruce had at least learned that it would not be good if he just let her leave, so he stood up and tried to hug her. Of course, she pushed him away and cried even harder.

"No one ever cared for me. My father didn't care because he left me and NEVER contacted me even one time. My mother did not care—by her own admission—and YOU didn't care for me because you went after Carol."

"Wait, I thought we went through that?"

"Through what? It was OK that you screwed my friend because I was not a good enough wife?"

"Did you ever think it was because you were a drunken wife?"

"I was NOT a drunk. I was lonely," she screamed. She was starting to get hysterical now. Bruce could see that he had gone too far. How many other times had he snapped out to hurt because he did not want to look at his own behavior?

"Wait, Lisa," he said as he tried to grab her arm, which she violently jerked away. "I should not have said that to you. You are right, I wasn't there for you."

Lisa was about to run for the door, but the last sentence made her pause. Bruce took the opportunity to slowly walk towards her with his hand out.

"I am sorry. This is not about our marriage. This is about your mother, your father, and your abandonment from both of them. Can you forgive me for being such a jerk?"

Lisa could only collapse into the nearby chair and sob. She sobbed for the loss of her father, for the loss of her husband, for the loss of her relationship with her mother and for the poor relationship she had established with her own children.

"I just don't know how to love people," she muttered through her tears.

Bruce pulled Lisa out of the chair and pulled her so close to him that they were one person. He was not surprised to feel tears streaming from his own eyes. Lisa had been right. He had not been there for her.

When she had left for her mother's house, it had been the best thing she could have done because, for the very first time he had really been there for his children. It was the first time he could remember that he had ever thought of anyone else before himself.

As Bruce gently guided Lisa to bed he said, "What's an Arcturian?"

"We'll find out tomorrow," she whispered through her tears.

VIII
THE JOURNAL
~What's An Arcturian?~

The next morning Bruce woke up to the smell of fresh coffee, and the sounds of Lisa making breakfast. "How can a woman hate me at night then wake up and fix me breakfast the next morning," he said to himself.

"Two reasons," said Lisa, who had silently entered the room.

"And what would those reasons be, my dear wife?"

"ONE, you lovingly held me all night long. And, TWO, I had an amazing dream."

"I do remember hugging you all night and greatly enjoying it," confessed Bruce. "And, I had an amazing dream, too. Or maybe it was an image because all I can remember is this big fluffy cloud-like being filled with tiny stars coming into our room."

"Hey, that was my dream, too. Did you hear anything, a message or something?" asked Lisa.

"No, but it seems as though I was told to read the next message in the Journal. But, first, I want to eat that breakfast I smell. Last night was intense and I am hungry."

"Yes," nodded Lisa with a faraway look in her eyes. "Get a robe or something and I will put our breakfast on the table."

After a wonderful breakfast, calm conversation, and several cups of coffee, they were ready to return to the Journal.

"I am reading this time," pronounced Lisa.

"OK, I'll clear off the table, and you get the journal. Let's read it right here, where the morning sun shines on the kitchen table."

"Sounds good to me," said Lisa. As she left to get the Journal, she wondered if he just wanted to stay away from the living room in which they had had such drama the night before.

"Good idea," she thought to herself. "I am ready for a break from drama, too."

With the table cleared and one more cup of coffee poured, Lisa opened the journal and began to read. It turned out to be the Arcturian's answer to Beverly's last entry. Lisa vowed she would not become hysterical this time, and Bruce crossed his fingers under the table.

~BEVERLY'S JOURNAL~

1-10-02

Dear Arcturians,

I think I would like to visit the Starship. Is that possible?

Beverly

Dear Beverly,

Wanting means that you do not realize what you already have. Not only do you visit the Starship, you live there. However, you have not yet fully connected with that expression of your SELF. You will soon. Then your conscious experiences of being on the ship will begin.

You will begin by remembering not the Ship, but the YOU who lives on it. Once you remember that reality, you will have your first stepping-stone into your fifth-dimensional reality. Everyone has a stepping-stone reality, in which they "step into" a higher dimensional expression of their multidimensional self.

Soon everyone will begin to remember, or live, a stepping-stone reality. They will also remember other realities in their dreams and meditations. However, the secret is to know that everything you remember and everything you imagine is REAL because *you* created it.

In other words, in your fifth-dimensional and beyond lives, what you think about, you instantly bring about. It is this final stage of ascension into the fifth dimension that is so problematic, because you must BE the master of your thoughts and emotions.

In a fifth-dimensional reality, your every thought and emotion is broadcast into your aura for all to see. Furthermore, every thought and emotion you allow into your consciousness will instantly become manifest. Because of this, it is vital that you gain mastery over your fears.

The two vital tools with which to gain mastery over fear are *information* and *unconditional love*. Furthermore, if the information you receive does not "feel" like unconditional love, then discard it and look for a higher frequency source. Unconditional love is not only the antidote to fear, it is also the firewall that keeps fear from penetrating your consciousness.

If you suspect fear, do not allow yourself to "perceive" your reality through your solar plexus. Your solar plexus will accept that lower frequency information into your earth vessel. Instead, we ask that you *recognize your feeling of fear within your lower chakras*, as everyone experiences their own emotions through their own body.

Therefore, it is best if you too look at all energy

patterns of that information with your opened Third Eye. Fear cannot penetrate your Third Eye; therefore, you will not be distracted by the perception of it. Your Third Eye will then transfer that message to your High Heart.

Your High Heart will then direct unconditional love into that message and/or feeling. Unconditional love will protect you and heal your fear. Yes, fear can be healed, for it is a creation—a human creation. Therefore, we ask you to begin to *think of your every thought and emotion as your own human creation.*

Blessings,

The Arcturians

~LISA & BRUCE~

"WOW, our every thought and emotion is our human creation?" exclaimed Bruce. "No pressure there!"

Lisa was silently wondering if she could ever gain that much mastery of herself. After last night's hysteria, she was ready to try. She would begin by calmly reading the next entry in the journal.

~BEVERLY'S JOURNAL~

1-16-02

Dear Arcturians,

It is Beverly. I wish to communicate with you again through my journal. Since the last communication I received from you, I have been seeing amazing images and had a very unusual dream.

In my dream I saw wisps of consciousness entering the body of my human self. Then the body that I was wearing seemed to disappear and I was just a speck of light, a center of conscious awareness.

My formless state seemed to pull me into an Arcturian Corridor, which I now recognize as a kind of home. My journey through this Corridor was calm and peaceful. As I traveled through the Corridor, memories of myriad third- and fourth-dimensional lives swirled about me.

I was then aware that a higher force was summoning me. Feelings of unconditional love and visions of multidimensional light surrounded and comforted me like a warm blanket.

I could feel my formless state becoming lighter and lighter as my frequency rose into higher and higher frequencies. It then appeared that I was serving as the guide to a female human. I saw that she was asleep; therefore, I could easily expand a portion of my being into her form to enter her dreams.

The woman was dreaming of one of her fifth-dimensional expressions in which she was aboard

Athena, her Arcturian Starship. As I integrated my multidimensional perception into the neural patterning of the sleeping one, I experienced myself as entering that body. I was surprised to discover that I could perceive three realities occurring within the same moment of that collective NOW.

First, there was the reality of my "Primary Multidimensional Consciousness," who experiences and overshadows the many multidimensional expressions of my Multidimensional SELF.

Secondly, there was the reality of the "me" who was wearing an earth vessel.

Thirdly, there was the dream reality of the sleeping human whom I had just entered.

By maintaining constant connection with our Multidimensional SELF, I could focus on all three realities of these realities.

Gradually, I became aware that this particular life stream, whose name was Beverly, would represent one of my "stepping-stone realities" in which I would be consciously aware of my multidimensional nature.

I saw that Beverly had dreamed of her multidimensional consciousness reality many times. I understood how remembering her life on the Ship made her homesick, so she usually forgot those dreams as soon as she awoke.

I saw that Beverly was on the cusp of returning to her true SELF, but the closing parts of any journey are filled with all the challenges that have been left until the last moment. I saw that this "last moment" was her NOW.

I also saw that she suffered from the many remaining conflicts between her ego and her soul. Fortunately, within that moment, she was at peace because she could feel her connection to me and to our multidimensional Starship.

The experiences of living in a polarized reality filled with separation and limitation are usually forgotten when she visits the Ship because everyone there works in complete unity with each other and with the living, sentient Starship.

I happily share Beverly's memories of the unconditional love and companionship on our Ship. Simultaneously, I perceive how we, the collective consciousness of Starship Athena, are over-lighting Earth. Beverly is awakening to her Earth life now. She has slept too long and will have to rush off to work without taking her "time" to get grounded and centered in her SELF. It will be a difficult day for her.

My dream the concluded, and as that dimension of my self perceived, I had a bad day and felt conflicted and ungrounded. Only after coming home and writing this into my journal have I been able to calm down.

Beverly

Dear Beverly,

You are doing exactly what you need to do. It is important that you trust yourself and follow your own inner guidance. We suggest that you meditate before you sleep tonight so that you can align your consciousness with your higher expression, who you met this morning.

The Arcturians

1-18-02

Dear Arcturians,

I had another dream last night in which I possessed a new skill, an ability that I didn't know I already had. I don't remember the details of the dream, but it woke me up to make sure that I would remember it.

I woke up with the thought that something new was coming into my life. Something that I had always thought was impossible. I was pondering about what this new skill might be, but I had to get ready and leave for a meeting.

I could feel something lingering at the edge of my mind throughout my busy day. Even as I talked with others, I was wondering what this new thing might be. I have to admit that at this point I don't have a clue.

However, this feeling is similar to expecting something in the mail. When I buy things by catalogue, I wonder when they will come. I know that one day I will walk up the stairs to my home and there will be my package. Then I am excited to open it, see if I like it and if it fits. It is something to look forward to.

Wonderfully, every now and then I briefly felt connected with the unconditional love of the one who entered me and told me I was to have a "stepping-stone life." I'm wondering if maybe this new thing that I'm going to do will be from the perspective of that fifth-dimensional expression of my SELF?

I had time during my workday, so I meditated a bit and could almost see the fifth-dimensional, stepping-stone me that I met in my dream. That expression of "me" was taller than my physical me. She, I think it was a female, was thin, with short hair that seemed to stand up as if it were an antenna.

I even heard that the name of this expression of myself is Kepier. I think I stepped into her, but I'm not sure. The thought that has been hovering in my mind was that I could *not* do it. I could not step into that me.

Why? Why did I choose to linger when I had the chance to do what I have always wished to do? Why have I waited to make the step that I have wanted to make for so many years?

I went home, relaxed a bit, went to bed, and got up early to go back to work. In other words, the third-dimensional me took over. I worked all day, and by my last hour, I was very, very tired. Somehow I drove home and went right to bed. It was only 5:00 p.m.

I then had a dream/meditation, as I was half awake and half asleep, in which I went back to stand in front of Kepier, my stepping-stone life. I tried to let go, I tried to step into that me, but something was in the way.

Finally, I fainted from the effort and awoke to find myself on a table in a medical area. Kepier was standing lovingly at my feet while several others worked over me. It felt as though they were raising my resonance.

Then the third dimension struck again, as I had a dinner engagement that I needed to attend. My eyes flew open and I rushed to get ready and leave. I thought of my dream/meditation while I drove.

However, once at the restaurant it was back to the third dimension again, eating dinner, talking with friends, etc., etc. I was able to get to bed by 10:30 and fell asleep while reading over what I had written about my prior dreams.

I awoke at 5:30 a.m. with a dream I had to write down. I will summarize the dream and hope that you will explain it to me. In the dream I was in a building that was the foundation of some Guru. I was told that I was not good enough to go to the next level.

The person who told me that was kind, which almost made it worse. The person seemed to feel bad, but still had to tell me that I was just not good enough. I was devastated and after the meeting I wandered, trying to find my way home. On my way home, I saw several tall stairways, one without stairs.

The first one I found I could not climb, even after I let go of all the "stuff" I was carrying. The other one, without the stairs, was too frightening to even try. The dream ended with a long, long walk home.

Beverly

Dear Beverly,

First off, we know you can see the issue of judgment, failure, shame and disappointment. These are third-dimensional concepts that need to be released in order for you to ascend. You felt diminished by the judgment of one outside of you, and the entire group shunned you as not being good enough. You were a failure.

The result of this meeting was that you felt so ashamed that you isolated yourself. At the same time, you did not believe that person's assessment, but you still responded as if you did believe it.

The first stairway in which you had to "drop all your stuff" is pretty evident. The other stairway, which was far away and had no stairs, was another symbol of your inability to get "home" to your multidimensional self.

You woke up late enough so that you did not have time to process your dream. But your feelings from that dream haunted you and forced you to remember when you were young and felt that way all the time. You thought you had cleared those wounds, but they are still there.

You are now at the point of fine-tuning in your process. You are also daring to consciously connect, become one, with your fifth-dimensional SELF on our Starship. The young woman in your dream that judged you was of course a younger version of yourself, when you judged yourself so often.

That "you" was trying to be nice to you, but did not believe that you were good enough. In order for you to take this next step, which is to fully connect with your fifth-dimensional counterpart, you will need to release all portions of your third-dimensional expression that cannot accept that honor.

You will need to release all thoughts of how others perceive you, as you are marching to the beat of a very different drum than most people. Furthermore,

ALL judgment and the resulting shame and sadness will need to be released.

The way home may seem like a steep climb and a long walk, but that is only true if you have forgotten that you are *already* there. You have NEVER left! Just as you awoke from your dream, you can now awake from your illusion.

You do not have to be "good enough" to gain what you have always had, as well as *who* you have ALWAYS been.

The Arcturians

~LISA & BRUCE~

This time it was Bruce who was trying not to cry.

"Bruce," said Lisa with a concerned voice. "Are you OK?"

Bruce could only shake his head NO for fear that he would not be able to contain the deep reaction he had to the Arcturians' message.

Finally he could mutter, "It was like they were talking to me, the Arcturians I mean. I have never felt *good enough,* and I am always ready to push away the next insult or judgment. I guess that is why I have been so defensive with you."

Lisa decided not to *say* anything. Instead, she got up from the small table and stood behind him with her arms around his shoulders. She said nothing when she felt his tears on her arms and hugged even harder.

Finally, he seemed to feel better, so Lisa said, "Hey, it is a beautiful day. Let's take a walk."

"Yes, yes," Bruce said as he stood up. Lisa realized he was embarrassed, so did not complain that he nearly knocked her over. She had complained enough. Now it was time for her to stop being so judgmental and give the guy a break.

In less than half an hour they were out the door. The sun was shining and there was a cool late spring breeze. Bruce took Lisa's hand and they walked in silence for quite a while.

Then, gradually, Bruce began to tell Lisa about his idea of starting his own business and to even move back down into this area. Lisa tried to restrain her overwhelming joy. She had grown up in this area and would love to have her children grow up here, too.

In fact, their school year was almost over and she knew of some great summer camps and park programs nearby. It was not that she was trying to hand the kids off. But, she and Bruce were saving their marriage, which was the best thing for the children, as well.

"Hey," Bruce said. "I bet there are some great summer programs for the kids here, and I know it is a great school district." He then stopped and stood right in front of Lisa. "It is not that I want to get rid of the kids, but isn't it the very best thing for them that we save our marriage?"

Lisa threw her arms around his neck and gave him a big kiss.

"What is that for?" he asked, grinning from ear to ear.

"I love you! And I love our family," said Lisa, as if she had just realized that herself.

PART III

Chapter IX
THE JOURNAL
~Fifth-Dimensional Meetings ~

~LISA & BRUCE ~

Lisa and Bruce did not look at Beverly's journal again for an entire month. They had a lot to do back up north. Bruce had to quit his job, they had to pack up all they wanted and dispose of what they did not want, and they had to move themselves and their children, Leslie and Sam, down to Beverly's house.

Fortunately, Beverly's house was very large, with four bedrooms, and plenty of room for the entire family. There was a nice yard that desperately needed some TLC, which Bruce and Sam were happy to provide while Lisa and Leslie worked on the house.

In fact, Bruce's mother, Joan, who had grown very attached to the children, joined them. Supposedly, it was to be temporary, but when she settled into the large apartment over the garage and made it into a cozy nest, everyone knew she was there to stay. Joan had been recently widowed and was very happy to make a move into a new life.

It was August before the family was settled into the house. Lisa had found a wonderful day camp at the nearby park, which allowed the kids to meet some friends that would likely attend their same school. Sam was in the third grade and Leslie was just going into first grade.

Once the house was moved into and the children were at day camp, Lisa and Bruce vowed to dedicate some time during the day to read the Journal. Joan joined a knitting group and a book club and made more friends than she ever had up north. Therefore, Lisa and Bruce had most of their daytime to read the Journal and plan their new life.

Lisa and Bruce had both changed in so many ways, and their marriage had improved so much since they started reading the Journal, that they vowed to read every bit of it. They had started reading the Journal to find out about Beverly, but they ended up finding out much more about themselves, each other, and their marriage.

The children were so happy to have Mom and Dad together again that they were on their best behavior. Besides, they loved their day camp and were both excited to start their new school. The children had been in day camp for about three days, when life settled down enough for Bruce and Lisa to pick up the Journal again.

The first thing they read was very confusing to them, so they opened their laptop to research some of the terms that Beverly and the Arcturians mentioned. It seemed that Beverly had also taken a break from the

Journal, as her last entry was on January 8, 2002, and the next one was five months later.

~BEVERLY'S JOURNAL ~

6-09-02

Dear Arcturians,
Since I communicated with my own higher self, I have been getting some pretty strange messages via dreams and meditations. I think these messages have something to do with my fifth-dimensional Kepier self and accepting my "new abilities."

I will add these communications to this Journal so that you explain them to me.

When I first received a message from my Kepier self, I was very surprised to have an expression of my own self who was writing to me via my journal, as if she was me. I mean, Kepier is me, but I forgot that me because it made me too homesick for my Starship.

I started the first communication by jotting it down on a nearby piece of paper. I will now add Kepier's introductory message to me, which is very confusing for my 3D brain. How can I be the *me* receiving the message, as well as the *me* writing the message?

6-10-02

Dear Beverly,

I am Kepier. I am within your conscious mind now, but our brains are not yet intermingled. However, I can speak from my consciousness to your consciousness by what some have termed as "channeling." Just as you communicate with the Arcturians, you can communicate with me. However, I will feel very differently to you than the Arcturians feel.

Kepier

Dear Kepier,

For some reason it is easier to talk with the Arcturians via writing than it is to you. Maybe that is because they feel much more evolved than me, whereas you feel, I don't know… NO, I do know. You feel like *me* on the Starship.

Oh, I am crying so hard now that I can barely write, but I will continue writing because I think I am uncovering a deep secret that I have kept from myself. I mean I know that David and I came to Earth from our Ship to assist the Earth humans.

But, I guess I forgot that I actually bi-located. I forgot that I left a version of myself on the Ship and entered into a human who was living on Earth. Oh, I forgot who I was and why I came here. Then I suffered the decades of sorrow and deep loneliness until, finally, I met David.

David was from the Ship as well. Therefore, when he helped me to remember *our* true self on the Ship, I started missing my life on the Ship. I realized that I wanted to return to the Starship, but I was also dedicated to the mission that I bi-located to Earth to fulfill.

I came to Earth to be among the ones who volunteered to assist in creating New Earth. However, I did not know how to fulfill this plan. Then, once I got married, I had a daughter and got lost in the hustle of a third-dimensional reality.

On the other hand, I was aware that there was a cosmic plan that had been in place since before "time" that included the ascension of not only the small planet Earth but also much of this quadrant of space. I also remembered that when we entered the reality of physical Earth, we had to learn about free will.

The fulfillment of the reason we chose to enter this physical reality is what allows us to choose to *log out* of this reality. We, as there are many of us, entered this particular timeline of third-dimensional Earth so that we could experience the intense separation of an extremely polarized reality.

It is only by returning to our unity consciousness with the ONE that the illusions of separation and polarization can be released. I am pretty sure that in order to consciously engage in the stellar event of personal/planetary ascension, the "individual" members of this planet need to unite into ONE Being.

Since we members of the Galactic Federation were taught, and can remember how to ascend a reality, we were chosen to bi-locate into earth vessels. However, we are not *just* the person that we appear to be in this life. Therefore, our transition may be more complex.

We have chosen to take a body on this planet within this NOW of planetary ascension because we have practiced this ascension event for myriad incarnations. NOW the dress rehearsals are over. It is Show Time!

Will we remember our lines? Will we remember to stand on our mark? Will we remember our part and the role we chose to play? These are questions that haunt all of us who are conscious of the immediacy of this event. What is the answer to these questions? What have I learned from all the information that I have recovered and studied?

Beverly

Dear Beverly,

I am Kepier, and am writing in your journal. Dear Beverly, you have written so much, remembered so much, read and studied so much. Now you have to pull it all together into a cohesive whole. In fact, WE—you and I—are one person resonating to different frequencies. Therefore, we must form a deep bond so that you, Beverly, can totally trust me, Kepier.

Beverly, will you be able to totally trust that I, Kepier, am a higher dimensional expression of your multidimensional self? We are ONE being. I resonate to the fifth dimension and you resonate to the third dimension.

I am not sure how to cross that invisible border from my galactic self into your human self. I can only hope you, Beverly, will surrender into the acceptance that you also volunteered for our merging, but your third-dimensional brain forgot.

I wish that I could guide you more, but I am also stepping into a great UNKNOWN. Maybe, if I start with remembering the future of when we are already on New Earth, I can remember how we created getting there?

Yes, I do KNOW that I am already on New Earth. In fact, I am confident that I have never left it. Is it possible that if I can remember how I bi-located here, I can assist you, Beverly, to remember how to bi-locate into New Earth, as well?

The answer again is "I don't know." However, I am willing to enter into this *unknown* and to share it with you, Beverly. I hope that together, we can blaze a trail that answers both of our questions.

Kepier

~LISA & BRUCE~

"What?" said Lisa and Bruce in unison.

"Oh, Bruce," said Lisa. "I feel awful. Did I upset our entire life to read the journal of a woman who is obviously schizophrenic? Talk about delusions of grandeur. My mother just straight up went crazy."

Lisa was so upset that she did not even notice that Bruce was on the search engine looking up New Earth, bi-location, starships, fifth-dimensional and quadrants of space. Whereas Lisa already felt guilty for uprooting her entire family, including Bruce's mother, Bruce was remembering every sci-fi book and movie he had ever enjoyed.

"Could it really be true?" asked Bruce, as if Lisa were able to answer. "Lisa," he said, "check out what I have discovered on the Internet about these topics."

"Oh, Bruce, there is all kinds of weird stuff on the Internet."

"Is any of it any weirder than finding an old woman's journal who talks about other realities? How is this final statement any different than what we have been reading so far?"

Lisa looked away, trying to stop crying.

"Lisa," Bruce repeated in a softer voice. "Honey, why are you really crying?"

Lisa was unable to answer for a while, as she did not know herself, but Bruce was patiently and expectantly waiting for her answer.

"Lisa, honey," he said gently (he was finally learning to be gentle when she cried rather being intimidated). "Look at me, Lisa. What is wrong?" Bruce continued as he softly turned her head towards him.

"Oh Bruce," Lisa began speaking, which made the tears burst forth as she gave up on trying to control her emotions. "Bruce, why, why when we are finally figuring our how to have a happy, loving family, does everything have to change?"

Bruce moved the laptop and the journal to the table so that he could hold Lisa tightly against his chest. He held her in this manner until she finally pulled away.

"Thank you for not trying to fix this situation. I know that we know about things that others could never, would never, believe. What do we do with this information? Who could we tell?"

"Well," said Bruce as he picked up the laptop, "look at all the articles I found about these subjects. We are NOT the only ones who know this. We are just new to knowing it. This information, along with the money that your mother gave us from, where?, outer space, has changed us. It has changed us down to our very core. If the information in this journal can change our family—and it did change *our* family—why would it not change other people and other families?"

"But Bruce," Lisa argued, "this is really weird stuff. How could we share it? We have children to protect."

"That is just the point, Lisa. We need to protect our children, not by hiding our heads in the collective sand, but by making a better world for them to grow up in. In fact, it is our duty to make sure that they even *have* a world to grow up in.

"Since I have I have quit my mind-numbing job, I have been researching on the Net everything that was related to the information in Beverly's journal. There is a LOT of information about all of the things that Beverly has talked about. And, we are barely half way through it.

"Lisa, we have an obligation to our children to make sure that they have a happy and safe world to grow up on. That is not how the world is now. I know you hate to read the newspapers, Internet, or watch shows on TV about the state of our world, but it is NOT good.

"Lisa, look at how we have changed. Where would we be now if we had not read this information?"

"Divorced," said Lisa as she looked at her lap. "We would be divorced and our children who are now very happy, would be sad and angry. You are right,

Bruce. I was just scared, but I am more frightened for my children's future, than for my own present."

"That-a-girl," shouted Bruce. He closed his computer and put the journal in a cupboard by the couch. "We are going for a walk. I want to show you something."

While they were walking, Bruce told Lisa about his ideas about finding a way to share the important information they received in Beverly's journal. In the job he just left, he had served as a project manager. He hated all the greed-driven projects he had to manage, but he loved being the manager.

"I know how to research, create and manage a project and communicate with the people involved," Bruce said as they walked to the empty office Bruce had seen the other day. "Therefore, Sweety,"—he had started using endearing words with Lisa lately—"I can research, create and manage a project that means something to me."

Lisa was starting to get excited too, but was concerned about how they could release this totally new information to people. "Bruce," she said. "I understand what you are saying, but how could we ever make them understand?"

Bruce smiled because Lisa had said "we." "I don't know yet what we will share, or how we will share it. But, I do finally have enough faith in me, and in us, that I know we will figure it out. Also, I have found where we will do it. It is only a few more blocks."

Lisa was so happy to see the joy and excitement on Bruce's face that she vowed to express no more doubts. Instead, she decided to wait and see. It was in that moment that Lisa realized that she had totally changed and was ready to begin an entirely new life.

Best of all, *all* her loved ones would begin that life with her. "How wonderful is that?" she asked herself, just as Bruce was pointing to the empty building.

Did Lisa forget to include her mother? Yes, just as Beverly had forgotten to include Lisa, Lisa had now forgotten to include Beverly. Lisa did not reflect on that issue, yet, but maybe the next few sections would alter the way that Lisa viewed her mother.

Lisa and Bruce still had time to read some of the journal. Therefore, as soon as they entered the house, got some warm tea and were relaxing on the couch, Bruce said, "Hey, let's see if the journal can give us some help about *our* project. Lisa, I heard you say 'our' before, and I am so excited that you thought of us as ONE person having OUR project."

Lisa was not sure if she was up for more reading of the journal, but after Bruce said he "was excited to share our project," she agreed and got out the journal. This time it was Lisa who read it.

~BEVERLY'S JOURNAL~

6-11-02

Dear Journal,

Beverly here. I feel like I must introduce myself in my own journal to differentiate between me/Beverly and me/Kepier. However, I am having a difficult time fully bonding with Kepier. It all seems too weird. Yes, I am beginning to remember who I really am, but my beaten down human ego self is dragging her heals.

However, just when I thought it was too weird to talk with a higher dimensional aspect of myself, I started getting a message from the Elemental Kingdom. I wrote this short introduction in case anyone, especially my daughter Lisa, reads this, so they may have a small possibility of understanding it.

I so hope that Lisa does not judge me for my life. However, if she does have negative feelings towards me, I could totally understand why. On the other hand, I don't know if it is possible for anyone to judge me more than I have judged myself.

Since my merging with Kepier there is something different inside of me. I can't explain it. Once Kepier reminded me how much I wanted to return to the Starship, I began to understand many things.

For one thing, I realized that what *I wanted* to do is not as important as what *I came* to do. I came to Earth, and into this earth vessel, to be among the many who took earth vessels to assist in creating

New Earth.

None of us knew exactly how to create New Earth, and the Arcturians simply said, "We can't tell you how to create New Earth, as it is to be your creation." On the other hand, we were aware that there is a cosmic plan that was in place from before *time* that included not only our small planet but much of this quadrant of space.

I also know that we entered the reality of physical Earth to learn about free will. I don't know if I have enough "power of free will" to cross that invisible border into New Earth. I don't know how to surrender to that which I can't perceive. Therefore, I will have to resort to my imagination.

Dear imagination, you are the part of me that made me "look crazy," but you actually "kept me sane." Therefore, I ask your assistance. Kepier has told me that "imagination" is fifth-dimensional thought. She has also told me that New Earth is a fifth-dimensional planet. Hence, perhaps my imagination can best be my guide.

Maybe, if I can imagine being on New Earth, I can remember and/or create *how* I got there. Actually, I do KNOW that I am already on New Earth. In fact, I am confident that I have never left it.

That is, I know that some higher dimensional aspect of my multidimensional self is on fifth-dimensional, New Earth. If I could remember how I bi-located to

New Earth, perhaps I could remember how I bi-located to my current Earth timeline?

I have so many questions, which I instantly answer by saying, "I don't know." However, I am willing to enter into this unknown and to share my journey with anyone who may read my Journal. If I can blaze a trail that answers my many questions, perhaps I will be able to help others. Kepier has reminded me that I have taken a form on planet Earth to assist Gaia's return into the Oneness.

Since I know that New Earth is free of time, I am endeavoring to write this section of the
journal using the inter-dimensional communication that Kepier has re-activated within me. This form of communication is free of time, place, gender, limitation, separation or fear.

I am hoping that this communication style will catch the attention of a fifth-dimensional being from New Earth who is willing to communicate with me, much as Kepier does. Hence, I am writing within the NOW. Within this NOW, I am hearing many loud machines from a neighbor who is building a new home.

This noise is reminding me that we are also building homes in New Earth. Actually, we are not just building new homes; we are also building new realities.

I look at what I have written and realize that "I" is third-dimensional thinking. Therefore, I will transmute "I" into the multidimensional term of "we." *We* are standing on a threshold of light. We are not aware of how we came here, but that does not matter.

What is important is that we feel total joy and unconditional love as we—all beings of Gaia's body—stand within the ONE of transition. Thinking and feeling in this manner is quite a challenge, but we are beginning to feel something unlocking inside of our ONE. Could it be the threshold?

In fact, since WE with each other, WE are ONE with the threshold on which we stand. We NOW surrender into the image of standing on a threshold, which is united with all this threshold has ever been, or all that it shall ever reveal. In this manner, we stand on the threshold of all who *we* have ever been and all *we* shall ever be.

We feel a calling to remain on this threshold, as it appears to be some sort of an opening, like a portal. We will remain here in this portal so that we can download, integrate and transmute all remnants of our myriad lives of *apparent* separation.

Yes, standing on our new threshold is transmuting all that we once perceived as separation into the unity of our NOW.

Blessings on Our Unity

~LISA & BRUCE~

Lisa was speechless after she finished reading this entry. She did not know how to accept this version of her mother, but she knew she could not read any more. "Bruce," she said. "Can you read now?"

"Sure," he said as he took the Journal. Lisa was grateful that Bruce understood that she needed a moment to take in this message. Bruce was starting to understand a lot of things lately. She had never realized that he was so wise. With that thought, he began reading what Beverly had written the very next day.

~BEVERLY'S JOURNAL~

6-12-02

Dear Journal, Beverly here again.

I am endeavoring to continue thinking and writing in a fifth-dimensional manner. I am writing this journal in the evening, as my day was filled with many creative projects. Having my day full of creativity reminds me that, "I AM creating New Earth." Creativity expands my consciousness and awakens my connection with my Kepier SELF.

Since I am NOW "us," (Kepier and myself) I will speak as "we." We know that this transition to multidimensional thinking can be challenging. Our habit of third-dimensional thinking continues to invade our consciousness, but we are consistently remembering to correct our thought patterns to remain calibrated to the fifth dimension.

Because we are remembering to calibrate our thinking to fifth-dimensional New Earth, our multidimensional perceptions are coming into our daily awareness. As we look around our office, we can see the aura of our desk, as well as a glimmer of the frequency rate of our day. We are remembering moments in our NOW in which our transition is becoming almost natural.

~LISA & BRUCE~

"We and Now?" asked Lisa with a frown on her face.

"Lisa, I think we have to read the whole thing before we can ask questions. I am confused, too. We can check the Internet if we are confused later," said Bruce as he continued to read.

Lisa was beginning to wonder who stole her husband and replaced him with a multidimensional version.

"Since we are feeling unconditional love for our earth vessel, we are joyfully allowing our physical self to rest and relax when necessary…" Bruce continued to read.

"Resting and relaxing is…" Lisa started to say before

Bruce gave her *the look*. It was then that Lisa realized that Bruce was looking for more information about the "Center" he wanted to open. All right, Lisa thought, if I don't want his open-minded, creative self to give up, I will just have to accept that he may be a bit over-zealous at first.

Bruce continued to read the Journal. "We are also remembering that our earth vessel is preparing us to eat lighter food. Hence, our eating process is a cooperative endeavor in which our 3D habits need to surrender to the needs of our transmuting earth vessel. Simultaneously, our consciousness is resonating to higher and higher frequencies of our multidimensional consciousness."

"My mother wrote this?" Lisa questioned. To Bruce's look, she replied, "Well, how would you feel if suddenly your mother became a different person?"

"Lisa, I think your mother was always a different person, and she is just realizing it in this writing."

"Yes, you are right again, Bruce. When did you suddenly get so wise?"

Bruce ignored Lisa's attitude, kissed her on the check, and continued to read.

"We are also combining our creative and mundane thinking in a manner in which our life feels very different, even though it *appears* to be the same. We are remembering to remind our wounded ego not to worry, as we are supporting it.

"Within our multidimensional musings we are able to probe into components of our third-dimension lives, which were once primarily ruled by fear. We are NOW unconditionally loving our fear and perceiving our journeys through the lower frequencies of reality as opportunities for learning and self-discovery."

"Who is this Kepier person? Can I get one too?" Lisa tried to override her discomfort with more sarcasm.

"Lisa," said Bruce, trying not to be angry. "Why all the comments? Are you starting to feel guilty as you are beginning to actually like your mother?"

"Bruce," said Lisa indignantly. "Why are you defending my mother so much?"

"I don't know. Maybe it is because I am starting to like her."

Lisa turned away in disgust. She was *not* ready to admit that she was starting to like her mother too.

Bruce returned to the Journal. This time Lisa refrained from interruption a bit longer, and Bruce tried not to notice as her body got stiffer and stiffer as he read.

~BEVERLY'S JOURNAL~

We are realizing also that all these musings about our lives are completely changing us and making us release our old habit of attaching our attention to the lower frequencies of reality. We are realizing that the many "symptoms of transmutation" of our physical body are diminishing because we are remembering to run our personal energy into the body of Gaia.

Gaia is greatly appreciating the higher energy fields of transmutation that we are grounding into Her planetary body. Because Her humans are NOW able to accept and love Her true expression of SELF, Gaia, Mother Earth, is able to increasingly release Her attachment to the confines of the third dimension.

Gaia is gradually righting herself on her axis, so that areas of her body once covered with snow can reveal new wonders of planetary creativity. As we are walking upon Her land, we are blessing Her body for providing us with this schoolroom. We are breathing our divine breath into Her atmosphere and sending our unconditional love to Her waterways and magnificent oceans.

We are rejoicing in the beauty and wonder of our glorious planetary body and are giving daily thanks for the pleasure of living with Gaia in the NOW of this great transformation. We are also forgiving ourselves when we fall into habitual third-dimensional behaviors and constrictions of time.

We are allowing ourselves to gradually find our way beyond the old habits and limitations and are lovingly accepting our processes of change. Most of all, we are happy to be free of fear.

As we are thinking within the NOW of the ONE, we are realizing that fear cannot tolerate nor adhere to the fifth-dimensional frequency of reality. Hence, we are remembering to consistently return to thinking and communicating from our Multidimensional SELF.

As we surrender to sleep, we are awakening to our myriad parallel realities and higher expressions of SELF. We are lovingly reminding our biological, computer brain to remember our experiences, which are being stored in our High Heart awaiting full remembrance of our multidimensional life.

Just as we flow through our awakened day, we surrender to our sleep, meditation, creativity, and all of our higher expressions of SELF. We are surrendering to the Planetary and Galactic Unity Consciousness. More and more, we are remembering our Galactic Families and connections to the Celestial Beings of Light.

We are actively awaiting further communication from these friends and integrate their advice into our daily life. Most of all, we are freeing our attention from fearful concerns and allowing the peace and joy of unconditional love to direct our attention towards that which fulfills our lives and satisfies our "reason for embodiment."

~LISA & BRUCE~

That was it for Lisa. "Who was that woman and where did she hide my mother?" said Lisa as she stood up and went into the kitchen for the first glass of wine in weeks.

The new, wiser, gentler Bruce watched as Lisa poured the wine in the first glass she could find and slugged down most of it in one swallow. It was then that she looked at Bruce to see that instead of being angry or judgmental, he was concerned.

Slowly, he walked over to her, took the glass from her shaking hand, placed it on the countertop, and hugged her. After Lisa had sobbed for quite a while, she whispered into Bruce's chest, "Why was my mother never like that with me?"

Bruce knew to just hug her more and let her cry.

Chapter X
THE JOURNAL
~Meeting with the Elemental Kingdom~

~LISA & BRUCE~

It had been two days since Lisa and Bruce had read the Journal. Lisa kept finding some kind of excuse, and Bruce knew that she was afraid she would get more upsetting news from her mother.

Bruce had just newly developed some degree of self-esteem, which was why he was letting his idea for a center sit in his mind for a bit. Lisa was right. What could he teach or share or gather? He needed some time to think.

However, he still had a strong impression that there was something in the journal that he needed to hear. Therefore, that night, after he had kissed the kids good night and Lisa had finished reading them a story, he went into the living room, put the Journal on the coffee table in front of the couch, and went to get Lisa.

It took some convincing, but when he promised that he would keep track of her emotions and stop if there was anything upsetting, Lisa tentatively followed him into the living room. As he got to the couch he turned to see that Lisa was not with him. He started to get angry when a small voice inside him said, "Is that how you keep track of her emotions?"

The inner voice was right. He turned back to find Lisa, who was in the bedroom, sitting on the bed. He sat next to her, put his arm around her, and silently sat with her. He could feel that she was struggling with her emotions, but tried to be patient. After about five minutes, she stood up and said, "Well, what are we waiting for?" and walked into the living room.

"Do you want to read, or do you want me to read?" Bruce said as they sat down on the couch.

"It looks like you were pretty sure you could convince me to read this," Lisa said with a smile. "I guess I need to be grateful that you are sharing this with me. I would be a mess if I had to read this alone."

"You are not alone. We are a team!" said Bruce.

Lisa responded by handing Bruce the book. They were very surprised to see that the next entries channeled through Beverly were from the Elemental Kingdom.

~BEVERLY'S JOURNAL~

6-14-02

Dear Journal,

I had a very unusual dream last night, or was it an experience? Either way, I was speaking with some semi-viable light-beings that called themselves "Elementals." Therefore, I will attempt to allow then to come through me, as they said they would in my dream.

Beverly

Dear Human Known As Beverly,

Within this NOW of your morning, we are sending you a message that will greatly assist dear Gaia. Actually, it is we who wish to assist Gaia, but we must first make a peace alliance with the human ones.

The Arcturians told us that we could trust you, so we are releasing our journal entry to Beverly. There will be an introduction from Gaia, as she wishes to explain who we are in a manner that humans can understand.

GAIA SPEAKS:

My loyal Ascending Ones,

I am your Mother Earth. The members of my Elemental Kingdom are powerful energy beings who constantly assist me to create and maintain my physical form. The highest frequency expressions of the Elemental Kingdom, who you know as Earth, Air, Fire and Water, are the Elohim, who are the creators and holders of my third-dimensional form.

The *Elohim* reside in the *eighth through twelfth dimensions* to guide their assistants in the Devic Kingdom that resonates to the *fifth through eighth dimensions*. The Devas receive the "Divine Ideal" of the Elohim and transfer these Divine Qualities to the Elemental Kingdom.

The Elementals reside in the higher fourth through fifth dimensions to create form for visiting life-streams who wear forms in the third and fourth dimensions of Gaia's multidimensional reality. The Elementals assist in creating form for fourth-dimensional life-streams, and then assist these life-streams to expand their form into the third dimension.

I wish to focus now on my dear Elementals who have been working very diligently to assist my myriad life forms to transmute their chosen forms into the fifth dimension. The Elementals are busily assisting my human, animal and plant beings to raise their resonance from the third/fourth-dimensional frequencies into the fourth/fifth-dimensional frequencies.

Eventually, humanity will also transmute into their fifth-dimensional expressions. The transition from the third-dimensional expression into the fourth-dimensional expression is not too difficult as it merely involves the expansion of third-dimensional consciousness into the fourth-dimensional aura.

Let me remind you that I, Gaia, see all my life forms as equal expressions of my embodiment. Therefore, my plants, animals, and humans (higher animals) are ALL equal in my heart. I know that my humans have been lost in the illusion that their expression is superior to the expressions of the plants and animals.

This misconception has allowed the lost ones to cause great destruction to my plant and animal children, as well as my land, water, weather and atmosphere. Fortunately, my *ascending humans* are gradually remembering that ALL life is ONE.

It is this memory that is allowing my ascending humans to assist me with my planetary process of ascension. Unfortunately, many of my human ones are still asleep and are continuing to damage my other expressions of form. My Elementals have been healing the damage done to the myriad areas of my planetary body, but they cannot keep up with the humans' destructive way.

My Elementals are now also assisting my ascending humans in hopes that these enlightened humans can heal the destructive humans. I will now allow my Elementals to speak for themselves. Like many of my life forms, my Elementals live within Unity Consciousness.

In fact, the only life forms that experience individual consciousness are my humans. This individual consciousness has been both a blessing and a curse to humanity and to me. Speaking for all the members of my planet, I say, "Thank you, dear humans, for your escalating return to Unity Consciousness. I, your Mother, am very proud that you still contain your "spark of individuality" while you are remembering to *also* embrace your expanding Unity Consciousness."

Individuality for my humans has been a consequence of my intense polarity. Fortunately, because I am returning to my fifth-dimensional expression of Unity Consciousness, I will no longer be burdened by the challenge of the intense separation of the lower frequencies of reality.

However, it is difficult for my Devic Kingdom to hold their forms steady while so many negative thoughts, emotions and concepts of domination fill my planetary aura. Fortunately, my ascending humans are remembering the creative power of their thoughts and emotions. They are also learning to balance their divine attributes of wisdom, power and love.

Therefore, before my Elementals come forth to communicate with you, I would like to thank my dear ascending humans for remembering the stewardship that they have vowed to hold over my body. My Elementals, who are diligently working to return my form to my fifth-dimensional expression, are very pleased to have the cooperation of the ascending humans.

One final comment to my ascending humans, please remember that you, too, have elementals within *your* body that are assisting you with *your* process of ascension. As you remember to cooperate with your own inner Elementals, you will find that your transmutation of form will progress in an increasingly smooth and loving manner.

My first Elementals to communicate with you are my Earth Elementals, the Gnomes.

THE GNOMES, Earth Elements, SPEAK:

Good Nowness, Dear Humans,

We say "Nowness" for we experience only NOW, such as all Elementals do. It is only through the perception of our humans that we experience *time*. We say "our humans" because we live in complete unity with the human bodies through which we flow.

We, the Earth Elementals, are often known to humanity as Gnomes. We have been engaged in healing the immense damage that humans have done to the body of Gaia, as well as to their own. Not only have the humans taken many toxic substances into their bodies, they have also put many substances into the body of Gaia.

These toxins damage all life on Gaia's sacred body. We will not go into the many ways in which humans have poisoned the land and disrupted the balance of nature because we are here now to thank you.

Dear awakened and ascending humans, we wish to thank *you* for clearing many of the personal and planetary wounds that have resulted from humanity's long journey through the dark nights of forgetfulness. We can instantly perceive the humans who are in the process of healing their bodies, as well as the body of Gaia's body, because they are accepting more light into their form.

They are taking in this light, which pushes their uncomfortable darkness to the surface to be healed, because they are ready to clear themselves to better assist with the planetary shift. We Gnomes can more readily transmute the third/fourth-dimensional frequencies of humanity with the conscious assistance from the ascending humans.

It also greatly assists us when humanity remembers to send their unconditional love to our landed surfaces, mountains, caves and underground communities. When we Gnomes are empowered by humanity's unconditional love, we can more completely work with the humans to clear the waste material of their third and lower fourth-dimensional negativity.

Our process of clearing humans is similar to trimming the dead flowers from a plant. Our beloved plants love every component of themselves and spread their life force evenly throughout their being.

When humans clip off the dead flowers, the energy that once went towards healing can go towards new growth.

In the same manner, when we assist humans to take in more light, we can also remind them that this light will reveal any inner darkness, which is usually some version of fear. It is VERY helpful to us when humans transmute their negative thoughts, emotions and actions so that they no longer create astral wounds on Gaia's physical body. Once these wounds are created we, the Elementals, must focus on healing them.

On the other hand, we wish to give thanks to the humans who are now assisting us by transmuting the damage that was created by humanity's forgetfulness and need to dominate. The reason why humanity was so destructive was because they had forgotten their own power.

Many humans forgot that they have the power to create, or harm, with "just" their thoughts and emotions. It is this forgotten power that we, the Elementals, wish to address. If you want to remain on Gaia as she transmute into her fifth-dimensional expression, you must remember that your EVERY thought and EVERY emotion will become manifest.

Fortunately, there is a threshold reality of New Earth that will still have a bit of delay between thoughts, emotions and manifestations. However, even in that reality you will NOT be able to *adhere your attention and perception* to ANY fifth-dimensional matrix if you fall into fear. When you fall into fear, your resonance drops back to the lower fourth and third dimension.

We Gnomes work a great deal with the Matrix of Gaia, which is much like the bones of your human body. The Matrix creates and supports the forms and illusions of Earth's inhabitable 3D Zone in the same way in which your bones support your earth vessel.

If the support system of any life-form is not strong, then the entire life-form will be weakened. It is wonderful, and so deeply appreciated, that many humans are performing healing ceremonies for their Mother Earth.

Because of your willingness to assist us, we ask that you assist us in healing Gaia's Matrix so that She can transmute her Matrix into its higher frequency format. We are also aware of the deliberate destruction that the dark humans have created on Gaia's body and of the damage created by the greed for more, more and bigger, bigger, bigger.

However, that is an issue for you humans to work out amongst yourselves. We know that the masses are awakening from their long sleep of indoctrination and domination. Every day, more humans are even standing up for their right to have a happy life and taking back their power.

Within the long dark night of the last 12,000 years,

many humans have suffered greatly. Happily, you are awakening enough that we can lovingly remind you to be responsible for your own thoughts and emotions. Please remember that your every thought becomes manifest, and your every emotion gives that manifestation life.

If you could see the many fear-filled thought-forms that we must "*clip* from the body of Gaia," you would all be very embarrassed. You are aware that you leave physical litter on the ground, in the water, in the sky.

As your perceptions expand into the higher frequencies, you will become increasingly aware of the fourth-dimensional litter that humanity leaves in the aura of their body, their home, their workplace and every place in which they lose mastery of their consciousness and fall into fear.

If you call us, we will assist you to remember that YOU are the creator of your reality. We ask you now, what thoughts have you had today? What emotions have you experienced? If you don't know how to answer our question, then just look at how your day went.

You created that day. If you want a better day, then BE the master of your own energy. Be conscious that we of the Elemental Kingdom are bound to create that which you think and feel. Remember to acknowledge and feel the power of your wisdom and the wisdom of your love.

We are joyous to see that some of you are beginning to transmute your carbon-based vessel into a crystalline based Light-body. Please remember that each human is ONE with Gaia. Therefore, as each ONE of you transmutes your own physical form, your fifth-dimensional elementals will leave your body via your every exhale to be inhaled by another human, animal, plant or thought form.

Yes, plants and thought forms do inhale. How else could they receive light? Of course their inhale is different than yours. But, you must remember to become accustomed to life-wearing forms that are very different from your human form. Also, as your exhale travels through your environment and into the inhale of other transmuting humans, those other humans connect with your essence.

Then, one day the circle will complete, and you will feel that "essence of your self" within a person you have never met. It is in this manner of sharing your breath that your carbon-based world will transmute into a crystalline-based world.

Remember that we, humans and elementals, are a team that can work as ONE to ascend *our* planet. Begin by feeling our elemental energy in your body. See us in your body, in your land, in your gardens and under your trees.

We are extremely grateful for those of you who create healing ceremonies and stand up for the rights of Gaia. However, we ask for a bit more. We ask that you remember that YOU create your reality with your thoughts and emotions.

If your consciousness becomes dark and fearful, you give us a lot of extra work to do. On the other hand, when your consciousness is filled with light and unconditional love, you assist us more than you can ever imagine.

We, the Earth Elementals of Gaia, thank you in advance for what we KNOW you will do!
Next you will hear from the Elementals of the Air, Fire and Water.

~LISA & BRUCE~

"Wow," said Bruce as he closed the Journal. "I am so happy that I can share this information with you."

"Yes," responded Lisa. "I am happy we are a team."

When Bruce and Lisa looked at the clock, they both laughed. "We better get to bed now. Our team is back to normal reality tomorrow at 6:30 a.m." They got ready for bed and into bed laughing and joking like they were newlyweds.

In the bedroom next door, Sam was happy to hear Mommy and Daddy laughing. He had missed that sound more than he could imagine. He knew that Leslie had missed it, too. Now maybe he and Leslie could stop fighting, too.

The next day, Lisa and Bruce got out the Journal and sat on the couch as soon as the kids were off to school.

"You know," Lisa pondered out loud. "When I was a teenager I hated this couch and thought it was ugly. But now," she continued as she gently touched Bruce on the arm, "I think this couch is beautiful, and I love sitting here—with you!"

Bruce put his arm around Lisa and looked deep into her eyes, "And I thought that the best thing your mother left us was the money. But now I know that the best thing she left us is this Journal."

Lisa handed Bruce the Journal as she said, "Will you read again?"

Bruce took the Journal and laughed as he said, "I wonder what kind of beings will talk with us today."

The "beings" were the Sylphs.

~BEVERLY'S JOURNAL~

6-16-02

Dear Journal, who will speak with me today?

Beverly

THE SYLPHS, Air Elementals, SPEAK:

Good Nowness, dear Human,

We the Air Elementals, the Sylphs, have come to speak with you this day. We are so honored to be able to have a voice for the ears of humanity. Always, we have floated past humans without you ever knowing we are with you. We have often whispered in your ear, and some of you even heard us. Unfortunately, very few could understand what you heard.

What we have been saying all these millennia is that we feel your breath within our sky. When you breathe out your sorrow, we feel sad and concerned. When you are frightened or angry we feel these emotions and wish to comfort you. Wonderfully, when you breathe out happiness we feel joy and wish to join you in your play.

However, our lives are at a different frequency. Therefore, all we can do is express the emotion and intention of your breath. We glow with your singing and wither with your tears. Do you know how much of your essence you release into the atmosphere with your every breath?

As Elementals we are bound to express our creations in alignment with your breath. We Sylphs are vital to the life of all beings, as we bring oxygen to the mammals and light to the plants. Our plant friends are aware of our service and sway back and forth with the power of our movement. Our animal friends are aware of us but except for the birds, they generally ignore us.

Humans have called us Faeries or bugs. Some have batted us away, and others, especially children, want to play with us. Many stories are written about us, which makes us quite glad. However, few humans are aware that we serve to clear Mother Gaia's atmosphere and raise its frequency whenever possible.

We love to do our work in the wilderness or where there are few humans as the air over many of your cities is almost intolerable. We take turns working over these cities, as many of us have perished from your air pollution.

There was a time when humans honored us and tried to keep their air clean, but then they withdrew much of their assistance. We wondered if it was our fault, or if the humans had gotten lost again in their greed. Our needs are simple. All we need is more love breathed into the air to assist us as we transmute the polluted skies.

For a while, there was great disruption from a machine that pushed our ionosphere away and caused it to collapse. Our supervisors, the Devas, tell us that humans are stopping that activity. If this is so, we are very grateful.

Many of our friends were lost due to that horrid machine. In fact, we Sylphs do not care much for any machines and wonder why humans can't make them quiet and clean like the big Starships that fill their sky. The beings on the ships can see us and even communicate with us.

The star beings on the Ships have told us to be patient a bit longer as things are going to get better. Actually, many humans are trying to protect Gaia's beautiful places, which will clear the sky and fill it with the harmonious thoughts of the plants and animals. Then we can get on with our plan to transmute Gaia's atmosphere into its higher expression.

Our favorite places are over oceans and forests. We can relax there because the water and the trees feed us with their life force. To be fair though, we must say that more humans are looking into our sky with gratitude for its clarity and beauty.

When we feel their appreciation, our energy is renewed to continue with our work. These humans are our friends. They know what we do for them, and they try to help as much as possible. They may not be able to control much of the pollution yet, but they can send us their love, which is so very much appreciated.

Even though you humans do not see us, we can see you clearly. Also, we can instantly feel your intentions and know the humans with whom we can share our Silent Knowing. We have much Silent Knowing because we are everywhere and can *feel* information as it resonates within our skies.

We absorb the many thoughts from all of Gaia's life forms. Yes, all of Gaia's beings have thoughts! Animals think. Birds think. Even plants think. It is just that most of the members of the animal kingdom, and all of the plant kingdom, think in a feeling, vibrational manner.

In fact, non-humans think in vibrational patterns. Most humans cannot read these vibrational patterns, but we Sylphs can easily understand them. These thought patterns in our sky are how birds can migrate and animals can find water or each other.

These patterns also influence the weather. Humans are unaware of how much they contribute to the vibrational patterns of the sky. However, many children can feel them. Unfortunately, the children forget this ability when they become adults.

In many other "primitive" or "ancient" societies it was quite common to read these patterns to better navigate the land and sea, determine the weather and gather information from the ONE. If you will listen to the sky, you will learn a great deal. Also, if you call us, we will assist you in learning to read these energy patterns.

However, with the chem-trails in the sky, no one can read them. We have tried to tell humans that these white streaks are not natural. In fact, they are laced with chemicals that are very hazardous for humans, plants, animals and us. Why would humans want to harm the sky?

The humans who can talk to us say they are trying to stop this problem, but they do not have any more control over the "destructive ones" than we do. Fortunately, we can see that there are new patterns of a very high vibration entering the sky.

We can see these patterns and love to rest within them because they are filled with love and joy. Our friends on the Starships and our Deva supervisors tell us that more and more of these new frequencies of light are coming into our atmosphere. We are quite excited about this information, as we are ready for a change.

We don't want to complain, but we are ready to pull our beingness into the higher sky. By higher sky we mean the sky that is of the new light. We have looked forward to this new light for millennia and eagerly welcome it. It appears that some humans can also see the new sky, and when they can see it, they can almost see us. We think it would be wonderful if humans could see us. However, some humans are very difficult for us to understand.

On the other hand, there are other humans who are our best friends. They talk to us and listen to what we are saying. Do you think that there will be more of these kinds of humans soon?

We really hope so, as we could use some help. The frightened humans are very messy and release the exhaust from their machines out into our sky to choke our plant friends and make the birds and other animals and insects sick.

If any of you want to help us, we would surely appreciate it. All you have to do is look up into our sky as often as possible and say, "Thank you, dear Sylphs. You are doing a good job, and we send you love and gratitude."

Do you think you could remember to do that for us?

~LISA AND BRUCE~

Lisa and Bruce were so enthralled by the Sylphs' message that they lost all sense of time. Fortunately, Bruce's mother Joan had peaked into the living room to see the two of them engaged in reading the Journal. Joan did not know much about that Journal, but could see the changes it was making in their marriage and in their parenting.

Therefore, Joan had gone out to get the children from school. Thus just as Lisa and Bruce jumped up to pick up the kids, they ran cheerfully into the room to greet them. Leslie was especially excited about the picture that she had drawn.

"Daddy, Mommy," she cried. "Look what I made at

school today," she said as she shoved the picture in their faces.

"Wonderful, sweety," Said Bruce. "What a great design."

"It is not a design," retorted Leslie. "It is a picture of a Sylph."

Lisa and Bruce tried to contain their shock. Slowly, Lisa began, "How do you know it is a Sylph, honey?"

"Because it told me," Leslie pronounced.

"Yeh," said Sam as he came up behind Leslie. "I have drawn a Gnome. I saw one on the grassy yard at playtime and drew it when we had art."

"And did your gnome tell you its name?" Bruce asked carefully.

"No Dad, only Leslie can talk to them. The teacher told me it was a Gnome. He said that Gnomes were mythical creatures, that they are not really real."

"They are too real," said Leslie. "My Sylph talks to me all the time."

Lisa and Bruce would need to discuss this, so they smiled and Lisa said, "Great honey, and you made such a beautiful picture."

"Hey," said Bruce. "How do you two feel about

going to the ice cream store?"

"Yeh!" said Leslie and Sam said, "Cool."

As Mom, Dad and Grandma followed the kids out the front door, Bruce and Lisa looked at each other and whispered, "The kids both saw them?"

That very night, as soon as the children were in bed, Lisa and Bruce rushed to the couch to get the Journal and read it. Maybe they could learn more about these Elementals so that they could be at least one step ahead of the children.

"The children will lead the way," said Bruce almost as if the message came through him rather than from him.

"What," said Lisa as she jerked her head around to look into Bruce's face. "Where did you learn that?"

"In Sunday School," Bruce replied absent-mindedly. Then, as if he just realized he had said that, he continued. "Wow, Sunday School. Why was I thinking of that? Oh, yes, now I remember. I always felt safe there. I went to a big, old and very large church, and my best friend and I would ditch Sunday School and scout around the church.

"How interesting that I am remembering that now. I even remember the picture in my Bible where Jesus was sitting under a tree and all the children were gathered around him. There is something about following him as if we are children. I guess it is the innocence that we lose as we grow up," Bruce said, almost to himself.

But Lisa heard him. More than that, she 'felt' him. She had pictures of that sweet, cute boy exploring a huge old church with his friend, and the worse thing he did was ditch Sunday School. When a tear rolled down her check, Bruce saw it and said, "Babe, what is wrong? Did I say something to hurt you?"

"Oh no," said Lisa as she put her arms around his neck. "You said something that made me see your beautiful heart. How did I miss that during all those years that we were fighting?"

Bruce hugged her tightly and whispered in her ear, almost as if he were afraid to tell her, "You missed that part of me because you missed that part of you. And I did the same thing. We projected our own pain onto each other, but then we could not heal it within our selves."

Lisa hugged Bruce as she had not done in years and years. How did she miss his sweet heart and great wisdom? But she said nothing, gave Bruce a kiss and reached for the Journal.

"I will read first. OK?" she stated/asked.

Bruce smiled in response, but it was a different smile. It was a smile that said, "I love you." Lisa opened the Journal. She could only take so much intimacy at a time. But as she opened the Journal to the place they had saved, she heard that thought. "Why can I only take so much intimacy at one time?" she silently asked herself.

"Oh look," she exclaimed, almost as if to halt her moment of deep reflection. "More of the Elementals. Do you think the kids had heard from this one, too?"

"Let's see if we can get the jump on them," Bruce smiled. "As parents we are supposed to know more than our kids, right?"

"In theory," smiled Lisa, as she started to read the Journal.

~BEVERLY'S JOURNAL~

6-19-02

Dear Journal, are there more Elementals who wish to speak with me?

THE SALAMANDERS, Fire Elementals, SPEAK:

Good Nowness, Dear Humans,

We the Salamanders, Fire Elementals, are very pleased that our communications have influenced the humans. Humanity has forgotten that everything is alive.

Therefore, the earth that you step on is alive with Gnomes, the air that you breathe is alive with Sylphs, the fire/light that comes from the cosmos and burns in your fireplaces is alive with Salamanders, and the water that you drink, swim in or travel on is alive with Undines.

Just as you perceive yourselves as live beings, we perceive ourselves as live beings. We wish to tell you about the higher light of which our friends the Sylphs have spoken. Just as humans need to expand their awareness of SELF in order to accept the higher frequencies of light, we Fire Elementals need to raise our frequency in order to disseminate this light into Gaia's Earth.

Furthermore, we are attempting to match our escalation of light frequencies with Gaia's other life forms. We do not wish to "burn" any members of Gaia. However, we are bound to download this frequency of light into Her body. Therefore, we also ask humanity for assistance.

As each human raises their frequency, they have the power to raise the frequency of everything that they touch, think about, love, or even hate. It is this last part that many humans do not understand. By sending hate or even anger to whatever or whomever you perceive as your enemy, you are actually empowering them.

What you humans need to know is that we live by

different rules of reality than the third-dimensionals do. For instance, third dimension polarized thoughts lead you to believe good is better than bad, what you love is better than what you dislike, and so on. We resonate to a frequency beyond duality and have no concept of judgments such as good/bad, love/hate, better/worse.

We know only *attention* and *lack of attention*. Whenever our humans put their attention on any person, place, situation, or thing, their attention is a signal for us to "add more light here." Hence, if you place your attention on someone you love, we add more light.

If you place your attention on someone you hate, we add more light there. If you put your attention on a good thing, we add more light. If you put your attention on a bad thing, we add more light.

In other words, if you do NOT want to highlight some aspect or person in your reality, do NOT give it your attention. If you DO want us to highlight some person, place, or thing, place your attention on it.

We do not perceive reality in terms of persons, places, situations or things, and we definitely do not perceive polarities. We perceive only energy patterns. When any energy pattern has a great deal of human attention, we add more light.

We cannot determine if this energy pattern is a celebration or a war. You may say, "Can't you perceive the love or the fear?" Our answer is, yes, we can perceive both love and fear. However, to us they are intermingled.

To our perception, there are many who are frightened by a huge celebration and many who love being in a war. To us, these are both energy patterns with a huge mix of emotions. Our Earth, Air and Water Elementals are more inclined to discriminate human emotions. However, to us, attention means more light and lack of attention means less light.

All Elementals live in all life forms, including your human earth vessel. Your breath carries a great deal of emotion, and your breathing patterns vary greatly. When you are afraid you stop your breath, and when you feel loving you expand your breath. Your flesh constricts with fear and expands with love. The fluid in your body has a constricted flow during fear and an easy flow during love. In your human body, we represent the firing neurons of your nervous system. We work on an on-or-off basis. Either our neurons fire or they do not fire.

We also respond to the different frequencies of your aura. When your aura resonates to the higher frequencies of light we love to enter into your aura, as you give us strength and power. On the other hand, when your aura resonates to the lower frequencies, we try to avoid being in your aura as you deplete our intensity and lower our resonance.

We often marvel at the shifts in personal frequency

that humans will have during the period of just one day. These shifts in frequency are very confusing to us. If you are able to have an aura that resonates to the frequency of violet, why would you ever choose an aura that resonates to the frequency of dirty red?

Don't you know that if you just give all your attention to your violet aura, we can re-enforce that aura with our added light? No, we guess you do not know that. Just as you don't fully understand our reality, we do not fully understand your reality.

Perhaps, we can talk more often so that we can learn to better understand each other. Then we could assist each other. You could learn to place your attention on only that which you want us to amplify in your life, and we could learn when you really don't want a dirty red aura and need a boost of higher light to raise your resonance.

If humans and Elementals could work together, we could assist you in creating your Lightbody, and you could assist us in creating our New Earth. Do you think that would ever be possible?

~LISA & BRUCE~

"Lightbody?" said Lisa. "What is a Lightbody? Wait, did Matria and Jaqual say something about Lightbody?"

"Yes, yes," replied Bruce. "I think that is a higher

frequency body made of light. Are we humans supposed to be able to have a Lightbody?" he said as he reached for his computer to look it up. "Yes, it says here," Bruce continued, "that our planet is going into a higher frequency and that we will adapt to that new planet by transmuting our physical bodies into bodies of Light."

"Thanks, I guess," said Lisa. " I am sorry, Bruce, but I cannot take in any of information right now. I am busy enough accepting that there a little being called elementals."

Bruce laughed and put his arm around Lisa. "I understand." He looked at the Journal and said, "Do you want me to read about the Undines?"

"Yes, but let me get a cup of tea that I can sip while you read to me," replied Lisa as she headed for the kitchen. Bruce closed his eyes while she was gone to meditate on the concept of elementals. Or, were they a reality? He was losing all sense of what was true and what was illusion. He wondered if he could talk about that concept with Lisa. She was much more loving and open than before, but she still seemed to have a lot of fear.

He could feel her fear like the Salamanders could feel fear. And just like the Salamanders were pushed away by fear, so was he. Should he talk to her about that? Were they close enough yet? Fortunately, Lisa returned just then, tea in hand. Therefore, those questions could be answered at a later time.

Lisa sat down next to him and began to sip her tea, and Bruce put the Journal on his lap and started reading.

~BEVERLY'S JOURNAL~

6-20-02

THE UNDINES, Water Elementals, SPEAK:

Good Nowness, Dear Humans,

We Undines, the Water Elementals, are joyous to speak with our humans. We say "our" humans because our element of water fills so much of your earth vessel. We know that our work is very important, as water is the greatest resource on Gaia's body. However, many humans do not realize that, for if they did, they would surely make sure that it remained clear and fresh.

Once, our great oceans and waterways were clear and pristine. There was enough life within our waters to feed humanity and other animals and still have more than enough water creatures left to procreate.

Now many of our waters are polluted and void of life. We needn't lecture you about our plight, as we know you are aware. It is just that we have a great sadness that tends to hinder our work of transmutation.

Humans use water to clean their bodies, their houses, their cars, their clothing and for many other parts of their life.

Why don't they keep their water clean? It seems as though we work as hard as we can, only to have another human cause another disaster, which spoils our waters again. Therefore, we wish to ask our humans to join us in clearing our waterways and protecting our marine life.

We are aware of those dear hearts that have chosen to assist us, and we know also that it is "the few" that are harming this great resource for "the many."

Water Elementals also flow through your physical bodies. Furthermore, you regularly drink our sacred fluid. If you could send love to the water that you drink, you would greatly increase your health.

Water is a template for life, which is receptive to thought and emotion. Therefore, if you drink water when you are angry, afraid or sad, you taint the water that you drink. On the other hand, when you take a moment to send love into the water before you drink it, you are actually sending your body love via the water.

Furthermore, if you send both multidimensional light and unconditional love into the water that you drink, you will greatly accelerate your ascension process. Also, since there is even more water on the body of Gaia than in your own form, you would greatly assist planetary ascension if you blessed all forms of water with light and love. That blessing alone would do much to clear our waterways and raise the frequency of our water molecules.

Elementals do not perceive your world or your behavior in the same manner that you do. We Undines perceive water as the force of all life. We see how our rain keeps the Plant Kingdom healthy and fertile. We see how our water clears the smog from the sky and the dirt from the ground, cars and houses.

Our waters have been great liquid highways that you have traveled for millennia. We see that water is serving humanity in many ways, but we don't see how humanity is creating a balance and serving water.

On the other hand, we understand that many humans are expanding their consciousness to perceive life forces that were once perceived as "things." They are beginning to remember that Earth is a sentient, living being. As the consciousness of each human expands, humanity increasingly understands reality.

Just as our perception of reality changes when we resonate to the slow frequency of ice or the fast frequency of a running stream, your perceptions change when you are no longer "frozen" in the time-bound structure of third-dimensional Earth.

As your mind expands, new ideas begin to flow into

your consciousness. These new ideas can flow faster and faster until they reach "critical mass." Then, these ideas burst into manifestation. In the same manner, humans are expanding their consciousness from being "frozen in forgetfulness," to following the flow of change, to transmuting their form into a frequency that is no longer bound by shape or form.

Your consciousness, which is often symbolized as water in your dreams, is expanding beyond its physical encasement and is ready to burst forth to freely intermingle with all life. As you flow beyond your former limitations, you free yourselves from the many illusions that have haunted you for myriad incarnations.

Free again, your consciousness can remember your Essence, which is as formless as our steam. You will also remember that you have taken a vow to protect life in ALL its forms. As you return to your higher expression of your SELF, your immense creative power will return, and you will actively participate in creating New Earth.

Dear humans, your form is created by the same elements and Elementals as Earth. In fact, our Elementals flow through you, just as we flow through Gaia. Hence, you are the Deva that pulls all our myriad elements into ONE body.

With this awareness of your innate powers, your higher purpose is realized, and you remember that you are here to be the stewards of Gaia's inhabitants.

YOU are CREATION in action. GAIA is creation in action. The Elohim, Devas and Elementals are creation in action. When you honor, love and respect your creations, you will complete this cycle of creation and be ready to begin your next cycle.

You will easily see the LIFE in All That Is, and become aware of the imprint that you make upon that life. While in your higher consciousness, you will see the higher frequency reality that flows into and through all life to unify you with the ONE life and our ONE planet.

~LISA & BRUCE~

After that powerful message from the Undines, Bruce instinctively knew to close the Journal. It would take some time to absorb the information from all the Elementals, so Bruce placed the Journal back in its spot and turned to Lisa.

"Let's take a walk. I need to go outside with the Elementals. Maybe they will talk to us like they talked to the kids," he said. He was half joking, but half being serious.

"Great," said Lisa, as she put down her cup and slipped on her sandals. "Maybe we will at least see them."

"Do you really think we could?" asked Bruce. "I was just teasing."

"Well, Leslie and Sam are our kids, who have our DNA. Let's go to the park where they saw them. Maybe we'll get lucky."

Bruce was not sure if Lisa was serious or teasing, but he was so thankful that she was happy and playful again that he added, "Maybe they will talk to us, too?"

PART IV

Chapter XI
THE JOURNAL
~Messages from New Earth ~

~LISA & BRUCE~

Lisa and Bruce did not see or talk to any Elementals, but they had more fun than they had had in years. They decided since the children could talk with the Elementals, maybe the Elementals would talk to them if they acted like children, so they did.

They went as high as they could on the swings, went on the teeter-totter, went round and round on the metal circular merry-go-round, ran up the hill and rolled down on the grass and got hot dogs on a stick. Most important of all, they laughed and laughed with innocent joy.

Joan was picking up the children from school, so they decided to take a walk around the town where their family would all live together. Bruce and Lisa looked for a new mattress for Beverly's bed, which had become their bed, as well as some other furniture.

~LISA & BRUCE~

"We didn't talk to the elementals, but being playful was one of the best things I have done in quite a while," said Bruce as they entered the house.

"I totally agree," said Lisa. "Let's check out the Journal before your mom and the kids come back."

"Great," replied Bruce, "I will read, OK?"

"Sure," Lisa replied.

~BEVERLY'S JOURNAL~

7-15-02

Dear Journal,

This morning I received a message from a person who said he was "creating New Earth." I had no idea what he was talking about, or how I was able to write down his message, but the information was so interesting that I just kept writing. I will call these entries, as I somehow know there will be more,

"The Journal About Creating New Earth."

Creating New Earth
Introduction from Bob

Hello, my name on 3D Earth was Bob, so please think of me by that name. I have a story to tell you, and I do not know if you will be able to accept it. The Arcturians told me that I could talk to you because they were talking to you. They said your name was Beverly.

So Beverly, I am sending you my story in the hope that you will accept it as true and have the courage to pass it on to others. I hope to meet you in my world soon, but in the meantime, maybe you can spread my story to others. I will begin with:

The First Entry
Waking Up

I wake up in the morning and allow my first thought to be, "I am creating New Earth." Before I arise from my bed, I look around my room to see its fifth-dimensional expression.

I feel the wondrous bed of Light and peer out the window to see an aquamarine sky with silver sparkles. There is no alarm clock here to disturb me, so when I hear that old third-dimensional noise in my memory, I smile and say, "I remember that way of starting the day."

Then I rise and go into my grooming room. When I look into the mirror I see the face of my Lightbody. As I bend over the sink, I see a lovely stream running through that room in which I can bathe in the clear, crystalline water.

I then go to my closet and see the new type of clothing that I wear in this wondrous new world. When I go into what would have been the kitchen, I tell my replicator what I want for breakfast and walk out onto the lovely terrace overlooking the fifth-dimensional landscape to enjoy my meal.

As I look over the scenery, I paint a picture of it in my mind, so that I can remember it when I go back to the third dimension. Yes, I still go back there, now and again. At first, I was running there all the time.

There were things I needed to finish up, people to assist in coming here and others to whom I had to say goodbye. When I saw how difficult my adjustment to this new kind of life was, I stopped judging those who decided to stay on 3D Earth.

After so many lifetimes of separation and limitation the total unity with all life and freedom from all barriers was difficult to believe and hard to trust. Happily, I am over that confusion now. I can't say how long it took me to get used to this place, as there is no time here. However, NOW this is my Home.

With my meal complete, I put the dishes back into the replicator to be returned to their molecular state. I do not need to grab a jacket or carry a briefcase as the weather is always perfect and work is not work.

If I want to experience a season, I can visit any planet via a Portal or enjoy a holographic experience. Also, "work" is now "purpose." I meet with a group of like-minded people, and we work as ONE to continue to create, stabilize and explore our new world.

Today, I am in a pensive mood, so I will take the airbus to my office. I could also take the transporter, but today I want to see more of this wonderful new life. With the very thought that I need to catch the bus, the airbus appears before my home. I run outside and enter the airbus. There are many friendly faces that I see whenever I take this form of travel.

We enjoy sharing our experiences of adapting to this world. Some of them still take frequent trips to the Matrix World, which is our name for the illusion of third-dimensional Earth. There are still many people who cannot open their minds yet to this reality. Therefore, no matter how hard we try to convince them, they refuse to believe in our world.

They call us crazy, and many of them shy away or are actually rude when we try to approach them. I think that is why I stopped going there very much. Eventually, they will open their minds, or they will "die" to that world and be born on this one. However, if their minds are still closed, they will be born in one of the threshold versions of this world.

The residents of the Matrix World are the in-between people. They have enough light to maintain a residence there, but not enough to raise their consciousness to this reality. They still need to have something "bad" or someone "beneath them" in some way, so that they can face an obstacle or be "better than."

We worry about those still on the lower realities and wonder if we will ever see them here. However, we are told that all of us have our Soul SELF in the mid-fifth-dimensional reality. Therefore, no one will be totally lost to us, even our enemies.

That is why we must stay here until we have forgiven all the darkness that we have ever experienced. Then, we can see the Souls that are always clear, even though they have decided to take the role of "villain" in the pre-ascension Earth.

Oh, here is my stop. I will talk to you more in your "later" and in my NOW.

~Lisa & Bruce~

"What?" said Lisa and Bruce at the same time.

"Somehow Mom talking to higher beings is easier to take than her talking to a person in some other version of Earth," said Lisa.

"Yes," responded Bruce. "I was just getting used to thinking about Elementals, and now this? However, I must say my curiosity is totally activated, so I am reading on."

"Please do," muttered Lisa, mostly to herself.

~BEVERLY'S JOURNAL~

Second Entry
My Life On New Earth

I took the transporter home because I wanted to get here instantly so that I could continue this journal. I have heard that we can communicate beyond time, so I am trying to send these entries to the time just before our ascension. Our teachers, who prefer to be called "Friends," are helping us to restore our full memory.

The Friends remind us that we can assist the process of ascension before it even begins, that is before it begins in *that* time-line. I have decided to create this journal so that those just before ascension can see what a wonderful reality they are coming to.

I am not a special person at all, nor was I special before my ascension. I was a young man in my early twenties just beginning to find myself. I was not particularly spiritual, but my mind was very open to the "shift," which I had heard a bit about.

I would not say that I had given any great service to humanity or that I was even connected to any Spirit Guides. I was just a regular young man trying to find myself. What I found was much more than I could have ever imagined. My awakening was quite gradual in that day-by-day I began to recognize small changes in my thoughts and habits.

Of course, now I know that my thoughts WERE habits, that I was actually changing. However, at that time, I didn't know that. I thought that I was just trying to adapt to a world that seemed to be falling apart.

I had a college degree, but it did me little good, as there were no jobs. The financial world was totally falling apart, and the weather was out of control. The thing that surprised me was that I was not afraid.

I don't know why I wasn't afraid. In fact, I thought maybe I was a bit crazy or some kind of loser that I was not worried about whether or not I could "make an impact" on the world.

I guess I was a bit of a kid in a man's body. However, I did have some unusual dreams. I kept having dreams of losing people. These people were in my life and, then, they were suddenly gone. I would wake up in the morning quite upset.

Often I would text these people, and sure enough, they would answer the text, wondering why I was contacting them so early in the morning. I guess they were surprised because I usually slept in. I mean, my job was of no consequence; in fact, I can't quite remember what it was.

I think that is another reason why I am writing this journal. I am forgetting that reality more and more. I do want to do something important now. I mean, my purpose of assisting with creating this new world is wonderfully purposeful, but I feel like I left that world without really doing anything for it. Maybe I am just feeling guilty that I ascended.

Our "Friends" tell us that guilt is one of the harder habits to release, and I can attest to that. They also say that all time is an illusion, so if there is anything in that last reality that we would like to re-do, we can.

I want to re-do the fact that I didn't give anything, yet I received so very much by coming here. I feel the unconditional love rising within me at the mere thought of how blessed I am to have come here.

The Friends tell us that our ascension is a birthright and that we don't need to do anything other than choose to come here. I guess I would like others who might see this to know that bit of information.

I would also like to share a bit of my process so that it won't be too frightening to those who are in the time-line in which ascension is just beginning. I was frightened, but at the same time not frightened. I know that may sound impossible, but many paradoxes happened towards the end, or was that the beginning?

I mean, at the end of that reality, but the beginning of this one. Therefore, I will call that process the "Transition." At the time, it did not feel like an ending or a beginning. It felt like a transition from one way of seeing reality to another. In fact, at first I was only "seeing" the Transition that happened for me.

Others would hear things, feel things or just Know that something very different was happening. I had always been a bit of a sci-fi buff, so my transition began with seeing "flying saucers."

Of course, now I know that that is not the correct term, as they do not fly and they are not saucers. They transport, and they are more like houses because Beings (people may not be the correct word) live on them, sometimes for hundreds of years.

Also, they do not move by an engine. Instead, they move by thought direction. They are in one area, and then the captain or engineer, whoever is in the Command Center, merges with the Ship and thinks of a location. Instantly, the Ship is there.

However, when I saw them on 3D Earth they looked like they were flying. Then, they would pretend to do so for the sake of the grounded ones. The inhabitants of the Ships, who eventually appeared after the landings, would think themselves into a form that was not too frightening to the 3D observers.

On the other hand, they could determine whether or not a person would be upset by their true appearance and would show their true form if that observer was fine with that. Being a sci-fi person, I thought it was cool to see their different forms, so they showed them all to me.

However, if I were standing next to someone who didn't want that truth, they would see a humanoid form, but I would see their real form. At first, I thought I was crazy because I saw things that other people didn't. Maybe that was why I could come here. I was not afraid.

Maybe because my life was so useless and devoid of purpose, I was able to embrace what seemed impossible at the time? The Friends tell us that our Multidimensional SELF is in control of our transition and will create whatever reality will best lead us to our ascension.

I believe whatever the Friends tell us, as their unconditional love makes me feel totally safe with their help. However, on 3D Earth I had NO concept of my even having a Multidimensional SELF. I was not religious or exceptionally smart or even well read. I was just a guy trying to get by in a very difficult world.

Now, the Friends have told us, all of us who are here, about our Multidimensional SELF. I still don't feel that SELF inside of me, but I know that I am in the process of fully remembering and expressing these many frequencies of my consciousness.

When I can fully remember my true, Multidimensional SELF, I will know how to move beyond this reality and into even higher dimensional expressions of life. I think, and hope, that writing this journal will assist me to go into the next phase of our ascension.

You see our Transition does not end with the ascension. In fact, our Transition BEGINS with the ascension beyond our third-dimensional self. Anyway, I guess I created this form of reality (I finally admit that I am creating everything in my life) so that I could give from this world what I was unable to give before I ascended into this world.

What I want to give to whoever reads this journal is that YOU don't have to DO anything or even BE anything special.

You, whoever you are, you deserve to ascend because you chose to ascend. I am just now remembering all the many lives I had on Earth and all the many things I did in those incarnations. I don't fully understand why I was just the "regular guy" when I ascended, but maybe it was to write this journal and to say that in your time-line:

You deserve to ascend simply because you ARE.

~Lisa & Bruce~

Before Lisa or Bruce could respond to that immensely profound entry, the kids came running into the house, with their grandmother just behind them.

"Mommy, Mommy, Daddy, Daddy," they cried in one voice. "We went on a fieldtrip today to the pond at the end of the park and we could see you playing on the toys. Will you take us to the park and play with us?"

"Sure," said Bruce after capturing Lisa's nod yes. "However, we are older than you and don't have as much energy. So can we stop off at the ice cream store and get a snack first?"

"YEH, yes, yes," cried the children as they jumped up and down.

Joan happily fell into a nearby chair and said, "I will fix some dinner."

Lisa went to her mother-in-law and kissed her on the forehead. "What would we do without you, Mom?"

Joan smiled and tried not to cry, as this was the first time that Lisa had ever called her Mom. She did not know what magic that Journal held, but she closed it up for them and placed it in its cupboard. Maybe some day, they would let her read it, too.

It was quite late by the time the kids were fed, bathed and asleep, but Lisa and Bruce just had to read another section of Beverly's Journal. Hence, they turned on the light above the couch and got the Journal. This time Lisa read.

~BEVERLY'S JOURNAL~

Third Entry
The Tunnel

I hope it hasn't been too long since you have heard from me in your time. I have no way of knowing, as we do not have time here, as you know it. I have a strong impression that my journal is being read. I don't know how to explain how I know things here, as I am just getting the hang of this "Knowing."

The Friends say that the most important thing is that we trust ourselves. There are no enemies here to be on-guard against and we don't have "bosses" who tell us what we have to do. We DO what we ARE. I didn't know what that meant before, and I still can't explain it, but I do Know it.

I remember how at the end of our old world, or was it the beginning of this new one, we all went into a sleeping-like state. Time seemed to grind to a standstill and, along the end of time, all our routines, duties, obligations and responsibilities seemed to have little importance.

We all felt as if we were half awake and half asleep. We would move around and do some small thing, like feed our bodies, and then we would doze off for another "sleep." It wasn't until we met in this world that we realized that all of us were doing the same thing.

It seemed like an eternal Sunday where our obligations were not calling us, but something else was pulling us deep, deep inside of ourselves. It seemed as if we were at the edge of a deep tunnel that was filled with a warm glow and a welcoming presence.

Later, when we talked with each other, we realized that this tunnel came to all of us in our dreams and/or meditations. There was no obligation to enter this inner tunnel, but the temptation was irresistible. At first we entered it shyly, like a young kitten moving towards a saucer of milk.

However, after we had gone just a short way into the tunnel, we woke up, without ever realizing we had fallen asleep. Finally, I decided that the next time I would remain awake the whole time I was in the tunnel. However, the tunnel seemed infinite and the light within the tunnel grew brighter and brighter.

Unfortunately, I could take only so much of this light. I had never meditated before, so I was unable to understand then that the inner tunnel was a representation of my journey into the Core of my consciousness. In fact, I didn't even know exactly what "consciousness" meant. The thing was, I didn't really have a choice, as the drive to enter that tunnel was so overwhelming that I couldn't resist it.

The Friends have told us that there were many people who did not give up their daily routines, and did not enter the tunnel, and some of them didn't even see it.

There were also many who could not believe in their own perceptions enough to trust them. Therefore, they saw the tunnel as some form of hallucination that needed to be resisted.

Many were experiencing these inner tunnels of light, but the ones who were afraid to think outside of the box were sure that they had poisonous gas or something. There was quite a buzz about the possibilities of great harm.

On the other hand, those who entered the tunnel could not believe there was any harm because the tunnel felt so warm, safe, secure and, well, loving. Since these love-filled tunnels were inside of our own imagination, which I learned later was my consciousness, we had the unusual experience of truly loving our self.

The best part of this love was that it was unconditional. We didn't have to do anything special or be anyone different or better. Luckily, for the first time in our life, we felt that we were perfect just the way we were.

I cannot begin to tell you how wonderful that was for me. As I said before, I was just a regular kind of guy. I had done nothing special, nor did I feel special in any way. Nonetheless, while I was in the tunnel I felt as though, I don't know how to say it, I felt as though I were ALIVE for the very first time.

Because I had to slowly adapt to the tunnel I would eventually "fall asleep" and wake up outside of the tunnel, but each time I could stay in the tunnel longer and go deeper and deeper into it.

As I went further into the inner tunnel of light the sensations began to change. At first they were soft and gentle, like a morning breeze. However, as I entered deeper parts of the tunnel, the light became as bright as a mid-day Sun in summer. It was then that the changes began to take place.

For one thing, when I went into the tunnel, I found myself no longer at the beginning of it. Instead, I entered the tunnel at the place/brightness that I was in before I "fell asleep." Once I entered this brightness, the sense of love became so overwhelming that my body was NOT the same body I was wearing when I entered the tunnel. Yes, I know that sounds weird, but as I continue this journal you will read things that are much weirder than that.

Before I close this journal entry, let me tell you what happened to my body when I was in that light. It is hard to describe it, but it was as if my body kind of disappeared into the light and actually became the light.

While I was in the tunnel it was as if I had no body at all. Then, when I "woke up" in my old world, my body was glowing and felt *very* different. At first I could only hold this glow and unique feeling for a few seconds, which progressed to minutes, then even as long as an hour.

For a long time I was stuck at the hour mark of being able to maintain that Lightbody, and I was getting frustrated. Then, after I had entered the tunnel more times than I could count I began to hear voices and see glistening forms quickly move past me.

At first this frightened me, and I immediately found myself outside of the tunnel. I decided that my fear didn't allow me to stay in that light, so I concentrated on overcoming that old habit of fearing anything that was new. With the release of that old fear of change, my process progressed exponentially.

The first difference is that, without the fear, I stopped "falling asleep." I began to learn that when I had experienced all that my consciousness could hold, I would will myself out of the tunnel. I learned this skill by mistake. One time, I was becoming overwhelmed and on the edge of that old being afraid, and I instinctively called out, "Enough!"

Instantly, I was outside of the tunnel, and able to remember every part of my experience because I had not fallen "asleep." Finally, I learned to accept that which I did not understand.

Because of this new attitude, in which I was free of fear and self-judgment, I found I could receive greater and greater light. Furthermore, the unknown light beings that had swished past me before, could feel my growing self-confidence and remained still at the edge of my vision until I was ready to address them.

Inside the tunnel there was no time, so I don't know how long it took before I found the courage to address them, but outside, in earth time, it was quite a while. Suddenly, one day I told myself that when I went into the tunnel this time, I would address these beings.

That was when I first met the Friends. Since that first meeting they have been my continual companions. I say "they" because they are of a Group Consciousness. Generally, they exist as pure consciousness but will willingly take on any form that makes us comfortable so that we can better communicate with them.

I feel as if I should take a moment here to tell you that my life within the tunnel gradually became the time when I was AWAKE, whereas my life outside of the tunnel became the time when I was asleep.

I walked through my mundane life as if I were dreaming. Somehow, I knew that I had to continue to play the "3D Game," and go to work, pay my bills, do my chores and see my friends and family. However, I found that I was mostly spending time with people within, with whom I could share my experiences in the tunnel, because they, too, had discovered and entered that inner tunnel.

We even got together in groups. We all went into our "separate" inner tunnels and found each other in the tunnel that we had formerly thought was just ours. First, we started in the room in which we first entered the tunnel.

Then we found that we could enter the tunnel anywhere. All we had to do was decide to meet in the tunnel. Then, no matter what time or place we were outside of the tunnel, sure enough, we would find each other inside our "own" inner tunnel.

At this point, the concept of separation was never the same. We were NOT separate from our tunnel friends even when we were not in the tunnel. It seemed as if we all shared some mental or emotional realm in some world higher above the physical.

Because we all had experience of being ONE when we met inside the tunnel, we somehow maintained a fragment of that experience outside of the tunnel. Of course, outside of the tunnel was never as strong, but we were releasing our old belief in separation.

Once we released our belief in separation, we were ready to address the Beings who appeared to live inside the tunnel. One of the first things these beings told us was there was NO outside or inside of the tunnel, for there was NO time or space to create that "separation." That statement was a bit of a shock for me.

Even though I had experienced that unity, as well as the absence of time, I figured that that was just because I had been inside the tunnel. Besides, the tunnel wasn't real, was it?

I guess I had become so enamored with the "meditations" I was having by this point that I never thought that I was actually moving into a whole different reality that was based on a totally opposite operational foundation.

The shift from thinking in terms of "time and space" to "Here and Now" was/is largely why we are in New Earth. The reality of New Earth appears much like our old life in many ways.

We appear to have separate bodies, but we do see the light that flows between them and connects us to all life. Also, the bodies warp in and out between Lightbody and a denser version of that form.

The Friends have told us that this denser version, which looks like our old form, except it is totally healed and youthful, is a temporary condition until we are ready to move into the mid-fifth-dimensional realities. Personally, I am not quite ready for that. Besides, I am really enjoying this world.

I am planning now, which could always change, to stay in this world, this New Earth, and help the ones in Matrix World to see what they are missing. Also, I feel as though I need to gain more wisdom, inner power, and I need some more work on the unconditional love of myself.

The Friends tell us that our full force of unconditional love, which is the Source of all creation, will only be realized when we love ourselves unconditionally. In other words, we can only send out as much unconditional love as we can accept for our self.

Oh, yes, that brings up the whole part about our Multidimensional SELF again and how we have myriad expressions of our SELF all over the Multiverse. But I will have to understand that a LOT more before I can share it with you, whoever you are.

I am signing off for now, but I send you my unconditional love.

~LISA & BRUCE~

"Do you think your mother is on New Earth—wherever that is?" asked Bruce.

"I was thinking the same thing. But also, I was thinking that we have really changed. I mean, here we are discussing whether or not my mother is on a place called 'New Earth.'"

"I know," Bruce replied. "But I also know that our entire family, which now includes my mother, is so cohesive and happy. Wherever your mother is, I cannot thank her enough for leaving us this journal."

"Yes, and the money, too," Lisa added.

"Yes, thanks Mom for the money, too," responded Bruce. "Lisa," said Bruce in a reluctant fashion. "I have not told you something and it is haunting me. Wait, before you get upset, it is actually about both of us."

Lisa sighed a deep breath in gratitude that it was not about another woman.

"Lisa," Bruce continued as he moved closer to Lisa and put his arm around her. "I rented that office that we saw a while back. I am so sorry that I did not consult you. I know that was a mistake, but telling you made it so real that I would have to do something with it, but I did not know what that something was."

To Bruce's surprise, Lisa kissed him on the cheek and said, "I know. I have a confession, too. You received a letter with both of our names on it, so I opened it to see if it was junk mail. When I saw what it was, I decided to wait and let you tell me. The good thing for me was that I did not get angry. Much to my surprise, I just trusted you."

"Then why didn't you just give me the mail?" said Bruce with a smile. "Never mind, I know the answer. You wanted to see how long it would take me to tell you."

"Yes, that was a part of it," replied Lisa. "But mostly I did not want to invade your process of giving yourself permission to start something new." Then Lisa put her arms around Bruce's neck and gave him a long kiss. "I am very proud of you," she said, then turned back to the Journal as she said, "Let's read the next entry. Can I read now?"

Bruce smiled and nodded yes as he handed her the Journal, and Lisa began reading where they left off.

~BEVERLY'S JOURNAL~

Fourth Entry
The Arcturian Corridor

I wanted to start this entry with more about our journey into the tunnel. As we all became more comfortable in the tunnel, we began to hear what the fleeting Beings around us were saying. It was very interesting, for when we shared what we had heard, we found that we all had a very personal version of that particular topic.

Therefore, even though all of us in our ever-expanding group thought that we were hearing the same message, each of us was being personally addressed. How can this be, we wondered? In response, we all heard the same response, which was, "Your multidimensional consciousness is fully operational inside of our Corridor."

At once we all thought, "Who is our?" and "What Corridor?" It was then that we first learned about the Arcturian Corridor. The tunnel was actually a Corridor through which all Beings pass whenever they move into a higher dimensional expression of life. We also move through this Corridor when we move into a lower dimension, such as being born on third-dimensional Earth.

In this manner, we met the first members of the Friends. When we met our Friends, who we later discovered where guided by the Arcturians, our transformations began. When we were outside of the Corridor in our "normal" 3D life, we struggled with doubting that our experiences were real.

Therefore, we exchanged email addresses and began to communicate on a regular basis that, "Yes, this is happening." And, "No, we are not crazy or making this up." I cannot tell you how important these regular messages were. For us it was so VERY important to know that others shared our experience and we were not alone.

In fact, more and more, the concept of "alone" was leaving our thoughts and emotions. We had formed this wonderful support group so that we always had someone to talk with whenever we doubted our process. As we moved deeper through the Corridor our process of transmutation (the word the Arcturians had used for change) became quite challenging.

I say "in our meditations" because we all still had physical bodies, physical lives, families, friends, jobs, responsibilities, and all those aspects of 3D life. However, we were becoming increasingly attracted to our visits in the Corridor and cared less and less about our 3D reality.

We were learning from the Arcturians, and other members of the Friends who communed with us, that we were ascending into a higher dimension of reality. Many of us, including myself, had great difficulty with that concept.

I had never heard the word "ascend" except to go upstairs or something. Also, the word "dimensions" had a very 3D meaning for me. Since I was always a sci-fi buff, I enjoyed the thought of other worlds and different kinds of life forms, but I thought it was, well, fiction.

At this point in our journey, fiction was becoming fact and all the facts of life that I had held so dear were becoming completely obsolete. The shift in my thinking was creating great anxiety until I finally got the nerve while I was in the Corridor to ask the Arcturians about my problem. I will quote them, as I will never forget what they said:

"Our dear ascending one, we wish to tell you that all the world is changing because you are changing and not the other way around. YOU are the creator of your reality, and because you have chosen to return to our Corridor again and again, you are becoming a

higher frequency version of your great, Multidimensional SELF.

"It is through the expanded perceptions of your SELF that you are able to perceive the higher dimensional version of Earth. This reality was always there. You just were not, yet, calibrated to perceive it."

That short statement summarized all the lessons that we are learning on our journey to New Earth. As we expand the frequency of our SELF, we are able to directly experience realities that were once only "science fiction." Therefore, I must share with you that I am not at the end of my ascension. Instead, I am at the beginning of it. *And, so are YOU!!*

Fifth Entry
The Light within the Corridor

I wanted to tell you a bit more about our experiences in the Corridor. As I said before, as we moved into the Corridor the Light became increasingly brighter. I want to add that, as the light became brighter, it began to take on different colors. At first the light was a soft pink, which made us all feel very safe, protected and loved.

None of us thought it was possible for a light to give us love, so we thought that it was the Arcturian's love that we were feeling. However, as usual, the Arcturians read our minds and said, "Although we love you unconditionally, it is the light that is sending you the love. You see, this light is 'alive.'"

Alive light was yet another totally unique concept that we had to understand. Fortunately, we were learning that if we just stopped asking questions and surrendered to the experience that, eventually, our questions would be answered from within. Because we were able to surrender into this pink light, we could feel how it was alive.

The pink light seemed to collect around whatever semblance of form we still possessed to create a sense of knowing that was superimposed over all of our questions. Then, gradually, the pink light morphed into a cozy orange light that felt as if an inner lantern were lighting our way into a new way of being, a re-birth.

Just as we became comfortable with that concept, the light turned into a warm yellow glow that empowered us beyond our wildest dreams. We felt wise beyond our years and totally confident that, whatever it was we were doing, was right.

Since there was no sense of time within the Corridor, we had no way of knowing how long we were in each hue of light. It seemed that some of us needed more exposure to certain colors and less exposure to other colors. But I must say that "color" is not the correct term.

It was more that we were in different, and progressive, frequencies of energy, and the color was the language of that frequency. We even learned that we could send different colors of light to each other, which actually became different kinds of messages. We were beginning to release the habit of talking in words and were learning to talk in colors and frequencies of light.

It seemed that all of us took a break outside of the Corridor before we moved into the green light. The green light was far more alive than the other ones, and we instinctively knew that we would have to prepare our consciousness to be able to accept it. We were becoming so lovingly united that we started to have the same impression at the same time. This gave us great comfort.

We decided to stay outside of the Corridor for what was seven days in that Earth time to prepare for this next frequency of light. At the end of one week, we all returned. How could we abandon each other, or this wonderful process? We huddled closely together and awaited the green glow that we saw emerging from the depths of the Corridor.

The green light was actually more alive than all the other colors put together. This light was, yes, we realized all within the same moment, this glorious light was Gaia, the life-force of planet Earth!

Gaia came upon us as softly as a falling leaf and surrounded us like a green dawn. We were warmed by Her light, chilled by Her depth, caressed by Her planetary love and enlivened by Her strength. As the green light flowed into our being, we were almost overwhelmed by the varieties of green that one Being could simultaneously emote.

We were the vast fields of early wheat blowing in the wind, the deep green of huge forests, the bright green of infinite meadows and the flowing green of fern-lined streams. All of the shades, all of these variations of manifestation of life flowed into us like the first breath of a newborn babe.

We gasped, trying to inhale this powerful life-form, and sobbed like a baby as we exhaled that great life-form into myriad shades of green light. Then, we were totally silent, each of us together, yet alone, struggling to surrender without becoming lost. As one person we thought, "If this is lost, then we are found." With this unified thought we fell into the green.

It was then that I had my first truly multidimensional experience, for as I traveled throughout all that Gaia had ever grown, "I" became "US!" I clearly experienced my every sensation simultaneously with every sensation of everyone in our group.

We were ONE with each other and ONE with Gaia!

Sixth Entry
The View from My Terrace

I am sitting on my terrace again looking at the vast vista before me. This fifth-dimensional scenery is special because it is a composite of what I see and how I see it. One of the things that we are learning in this higher dimensional reality is how much our state of consciousness influences how we perceive reality.

This topic about the perception of reality comes to my mind now because I was just thinking of some friends who chose not to join us. While I was in the Corridor with my group, I didn't miss anyone from my old life. It was as if I had died, but I also knew I was alive.

On the other hand, some people "died to me," not because they died, but because they chose not to join me/us on New Earth. I went back to Matrix World as many times as I could to try to awaken some of the people I cared about, as well as others I had never met.

Some awoke and chose to ascend to New Earth, but some never did awaken for as long as I knew them. I know that they are in the 3D Earth, which is actually a holographic matrix, but they believe it is real. Therefore, to them, it IS real. However, it can't be real to me anymore because I have been through the Corridor.

I remember now, I left off my story with our integration of the Green Light. Just as we prepared for seven Earth days to accept the frequency of the green light, we took seven Earth days outside the

Corridor to integrate the planetary life force of that light into our consciousness.

I say "consciousness" instead of body because we were becoming increasingly detached from our physical earth vessel. We were remembering and becoming a much higher frequency of being. This being encompassed our earth vessel, but was not limited by it. In fact, our earth vessel was now perceived as the anchor that kept our consciousness connected to physical Earth.

When we met in the Corridor again, there were many more of us. In fact, there were so many of us that we could not perceive any portion of the Corridor that was not occupied by awakening ones. The Arcturians told us that because we are all ONE when the life force of the green light entered us, it also entered every ONE everywhere who could allow themselves to perceive it.

The love and unity of that life force that filled the Corridor was so powerful that we became ONE Being with many versions of expression. That was my first experience of how it would feel on New Earth.

After the Arcturians congratulated us, we settled in to accept what we knew would be a Blue Light. This time, the light didn't gradually come into us. Instead, it was suddenly there, as the sky is there whenever you go outside or look out a window.

Whereas the green Light was a bit overwhelming, the Blue Light was like a breath of fresh air. As one person, we inhaled this frequency, which immediately activated a flow of creativity beyond what we had ever known. This creativity activated a completely different manner of thinking.

Therefore, our perceptions became increasingly complex as many possible versions of reality intermingled like clouds in a clear sky. In fact, when we looked at each other we saw myriad potentials of expression that we each carried within our consciousness.

It was then that the Corridor appeared to become much larger, as if to contain the many versions of our self. This blue light was so easily embraced that we were immediately ready to move into the next light. Little did we know, how different that experience would be.

Seventh Entry
The Indigo Light

The Indigo Light did not come to us from within the Corridor. It came to us from within our self. At first we all saw a tiny speck of indigo light in the center of our forehead, between our eyes. At first, I thought I was seeing things, which indeed I was.

However, I was still addicted to the third-dimensional thinking in which the world was "outside" of me. Therefore, when I saw something apparently coming from inside of me, I was quite confused. This confusion mounted as the indigo light became larger and brighter.

I tried to look around the Corridor to see what the others were experiencing, but I saw them "inside" of me. I don't know how to explain this experience to those who still think third-dimensionally, but I will try.

My experience was that all of reality was inside the Corridor—that was inside of the indigo light—that was inside of me. Furthermore, at the same time, I was inside the indigo light—that was inside the Corridor—that was inside of all of us—who were now ONE Being.

This sensation was so disorienting that I became incredibly dizzy, and felt constantly on the edge of passing out. But, what would it mean to pass out when I was inside of everyone who was inside of me?

My mind became so boggled by the experience that it took great concentration to stay within the Corridor. I had not come this far to pull out now. Therefore, I held on tenaciously, but was not sure what I was holding on to. Maybe I was just holding on to staying conscious.

At the moment of that thought, I realized how much of my life I had spent in an unconscious manner. I was sleep walking while I went to school, went to my boring job, had beer with my friends, saw a ballgame, etc., etc.

My entire life was a series of meaningless situations. To make it worse, I continually lied to myself that everything was just cool. That is, until I woke up. The waking up was when I first entered the "tunnel," which was what I called it then.

In the midst of my commiserations, the indigo light bored deeper into my mind. Or was it OUR mind? Then, suddenly, I was gone. I mean, I was gone because I had no body. I know I was there because I could still see the indigo light, but I could not see my body or the bodies of the others.

In fact, there were no "others." There was only the indigo light, but I could still FEEL the consciousness of all the ones I had come to know and, yes, love. It was then that I realized that the love I had so desperately sought before was everywhere.

I would like to say within me and within the Light, but they were the same. And neither the Light nor I had any form at all.

There was only freedom, love and, yes, there was joy.

~LISA & BRUCE~

Lisa was so moved by the last entry that she closed the Journal. Lisa and Bruce were so entranced by the story that Lisa had just kept reading, while Bruce had closed his eyes to more deeply experience this story.

Or, maybe it was not just a story. What if this was a real event? It was not until they closed the Journal and talked about what they had read that they realized that they, too, had joined some form of unity consciousness.

They jointly decided that they would also take seven days before they continued their reading. They wanted to fully integrate their experience, just as Bob and the group in the Corridor had done. Therefore, Lisa put the Journal back into the cupboard.

They also agreed that they would set the alarm and get up before everyone else to sit inside of the different colors of light. When they went to bed that night they set their alarm for 4:00 a.m. They were equally surprised at the degree of commitment that they chose, together, in order to follow this process.

At 4:00 a.m. the next morning the alarm buzzed and Bruce instantly shut it off so the children would not wake up. They decided to sit up on the bed and face each other as they both focused on a pink light. To their surprise, they both "felt," as they could not yet "see" the pink light. However, as they focused their attention on the "feeling" of the pink light, they began to actually see it. In fact, the pink light slowly flowed between them and around them.

Just when they were fully surrendering to this light they heard, "Mommy, Daddy, what is that pink light?" Their eyes flew open and their heads turned to the source of the sound, which was Sam, who was holding his sister's hand. Lisa and Bruce looked at each other for a moment of nonverbal communication.

Then Bruce said, "Mommy and I are meditating. Do you want to join us?"

Instantly, both Sam and Leslie were on the bed sitting in a circle. It felt so cozy, the Lisa told everyone to hold hands, which was very powerful. They sat together within the pink light for what appeared to be hours.

When the children began to squirm, Lisa opened her eyes to see that it had only been about 10 minutes. Everyone else opened their eyes seconds after Lisa. Sam, in his great wisdom, said, "Wow, that pink light felt just like love."

Their family meditation was so successful that they decided to do one meditation a week. Then they could all practice being inside the different colored lights. They decided that since the children were joining them, it was best to do the family meditation on Sunday.

The week after the "pink meditation," which was Leslie's name for the family meditation, was amazing loving. The children did not fight, nor did the parents.

Before the second meditation Joan said at the dinner table, "Leslie told me about the weekly meditation. Can I join you, too?"

"Of course," they all said in one voice, which made tears roll down Joan's face. To everyone's surprise, Lisa was the one to stand up, walk over to Joan, put her arm around Joan's shoulder, and kiss her on the check. "We love you, Mom," she said.

"Me too," said the kids.

"Me too," said Bruce.

It was just a few days later that the family, which now included Joan, met at 4:00 a.m. Sunday morning to meditate on the orange light. The one who seemed to understand the concept of meditation the most was Sam, so he led the group in visualizing an orange light swirling around the room.

Sam seemed to suddenly be adult in the way in which he directed the meditation. He softly talked about how the orange light swirled around each person then around the group of five who were sitting in a circle on the floor of the master bedroom.

When the meditation ended, everyone hugged. Again they agreed not to talk about the meditation but to wait and see how the orange light affected them. At first everyone stayed alone to get accustomed to the strange feeling they all experienced after the meditation.

Then everyone seemed to get more emotional. The first couple of days were a challenge, as everyone seemed to be fighting about something. But by the third day the fighting stopped and everyone started sharing their emotions.

It seemed that once everyone had a chance to talk about what was bothering them they actually felt closer. The dinner table conversations became more animated, the kids started really enjoying each other's company and Lisa and Bruce were laughing together in way they had not done in years. Even Joan spent more time in the big house visiting with the family.

It was after the yellow light meditation that they all started to change. It was as if they found the courage to do what they wanted. Sam had borrowed a drum pad and some sticks form his school and began drumming out some rhythms.

Leslie started singing along with her iPad music, Joan started selling some of the sweaters and blankets she had made, and Bruce began to decorate the office.

Since we started meditating with the family I have started to just know things," Lisa said to Bruce.

"Yes, everyone seems to be getting more creative in some way. I am not sure yet how I have changed, but I am sure you will tell me," replied Bruce.

Lisa smiled to herself and gave him a kiss on the check.

"What is that for?" asked Bruce.

Lisa smiled again and went to get the kids ready for bed. The next meditation was the green light meditation. Much as Bob had said, there was something that felt very important about the green light. The next morning they were in a circle on Lisa and Bruce's bedroom floor ready to meditate.

When they focused on the green light they all starting squirming and feeling uncomfortable. Later, they realized that they all felt a sense of expectation as if something was going to happen. They did not know what that thing was, but it felt like they would do it together.

Suddenly Sam said, "Let's fix up this old house."

Everyone suddenly opened their eyes as Leslie said, "I want my room to be pink."

"Can we all paint the house together?" said Sam.

"Yes," said Joan. "Let's fix up the house. I would love to make some new curtains."

"I volunteer to fix up that back yard. It is a weed garden now," added Bruce.

It was then that tears began to fall down Lisa's face until she began to really cry. Everyone gathered around her until she was ready to talk. When she stopped crying Lisa said, "Where is my mother? Now that I have this wonderful sense of family around me, I can realize how much I really miss my mother."

"Me too," said Leslie and Sam in one voice while Bruce put his arm around his wife. Joan comforted the children who were also starting to cry.

"The answer to my mother's disappearance is in the Journal. We need to start reading it again," whispered Lisa to Bruce.

"Maybe we can go through Grandma's drawers and see if there are any clues," said Sam.

"Yes, that is a good idea," said Lisa, "But I have one of my feelings that the answer is in Bob's story."

Once she said that, she realized that she had to fill the kids and Joan in on the Journal and on Bob's story of New Earth. "I am feeling a sense of urgency, like something will happen soon. Can we meditate again tomorrow? Bob said the blue light was very calming, and I could stand that right now."

Everyone agreed to meet the next day for the blue meditation. Sure enough, it was a very calming meditation, which they all needed as they had "caught" Lisa's "sense of urgency" and felt like they had to hurry.

The blue meditation did calm them all down, and they had a wonderful family conversation about fixing up the house and finding Beverly. Somehow fixing up the house seemed important to everyone. Perhaps it was the color meditations.

That afternoon, they went to the paint store to get paint samples to decide which rooms would be which colors. When they got home they had great fun trying different colors in different rooms. That night they all fell into bed and slept happily and soundly.

That is, except for Lisa. She could not get over the feeling that it was important to find out about her mother. Therefore, even though it was late, Lisa returned to the living room and got out the Journal.

She was just settling in when Bruce sat down next to her and said, "Do you want me to read, honey?"

Trying not to cry, Lisa handed Bruce the Journal and slipped her arm through his.

Chapter XII
THE JOURNAL
~Living New Earth Messages ~

~LISA & BRUCE~

Bruce was just starting to read the Journal when Leslie and Sam came into the room rubbing their sleepy eyes. "We want to hear, too," they said in tandem. Before Bruce and Lisa could respond, Joan entered the room with a cup of tea she had made in her room. "Yes, me too," she announced as she sat down in the big chair across from Lisa and Bruce.

In response, Lisa's tears became sobs. "Why are you crying, Mommy?" asked the kids as they got up to comfort her.

"Because I am so happy," she replied. "All my life I felt so alone inside myself that even when I had this wonderful family I could not recognize that I was so deeply loved."

Joan smiled from across the room as she watched her family huddled together to comfort Lisa. She, too, had to wipe away some tears and wished her deceased husband could join in on this beautiful moment.

"Thank you, I love all of you so very much," said Lisa as she glanced at Joan to include her as well. "I guess there are some things even more important than sleep. Why don't you guys jump up on the couch with us," she said as she grabbed the afghan Joan had knitted to cover the children.

With the children tucked in and Joan sipping her tea, Bruce smiled brightly, kissed Lisa again in the check and began to read the Journal.

~BEVERLY'S JOURNAL~

Eighth Entry
The Violet Light
Bob continues his story…

Eventually, I could no longer remain conscious within the Indigo Light and I returned to the physical world with a jolt, with the message of "Dividing of the Worlds" in my mind. At that time, I had no idea what those words meant until I showered, ate, and stepped outside. I could hardly maintain consciousness for everywhere I looked I saw two, or more, versions of reality.

I blinked my eyes again and again, but these were not the eyes I was looking through. I was looking at the world through my forehead. I later learned that I was looking through my Third Eye, which is exactly what it felt like. To make matters even more confusing, if I sat or stood still, I could see things through the side of my head and even through the back of my head. Therefore, at first, I did NOT remain still. I tried to busy myself with myriad mundane tasks to ignore this new experience.

At the time, I had no way of knowing that this "new experience" was actually a great gift. This gift was much like getting a new car when I did not know how to drive. Whenever I allowed my consciousness to rise above mundane tasks, I began to see two, or three, or even more realities intermingled into one.

Then, I would crash into things, knock things over, and stumble around. I had to call in sick to work and isolate myself from my friends. How could I explain this "condition" to anyone? Finally, I learned that if I closed my physical eyes, I could see through only my Third Eye. That is when it started to be amazing.

I could look out my window and see two or three energy fields merging into one or pulling apart from each other. I didn't know at the time, at least not at first, that those energy fields were possible realities.

Then, gradually, I began to realize that if I stared into only one of these energy fields, with my physical eyes closed, shapes, pictures and activities would gradually take form. That is when I could see that the landings were beginning.

The "landings" meant the landing of the Space Ships. Of course, they didn't exactly land. They hovered. Then suddenly, they would take off in a flash at an impossible angle of turn. Or they would just disappear.

The Ship was there, and then it wasn't. At first, everyone ran out and filmed the Ships with their phones and posted them on YouTube. But, eventually, the Ships became normal, like clouds. Some days there were a lot of Ships. In fact, they would practically fill the sky.

Then, on other days, or even weeks, there would be no Ships at all. It was then that we began to realize that we actually missed them when they were gone too long. In fact, we would get depressed or angry or lonely. It took us a while to figure it out, but the Ships gave us something.

When the Ships were in the sky we felt protected, which was very important. By that time, the entire world was turning upside down. It seemed that everything that had once been important was now obsolete.

Also, people stopped caring about doing all their mundane tasks. Money was so unreliable that we didn't fret over paying bills. Jobs were so scarce that those who were unemployed stopped looking, and, some of us who had a mundane job going nowhere, like me, simply quit.

How could I quit my job when work was so hard to find? It had to do with the Ships. We all started having dreams about being on the Ships, working on the Ships and being instructed about how to operate the Ships. It was so fascinating that we all hurried off home to go to bed so we could have another dream.

Then we began to dream that the Ships were actually landing, and, sure enough, shortly after that they started to land. We were not surprised at all, as we had been warned in our "sleep." However, one of the first things they told us when we were awake was that we were never dreaming. Instead, we had been visiting them on our higher frequency astral body. We had NO idea what that meant.

~LISA & BRUCE~

"Do you think Grandma is on a spaceship?" Sam said. The adults laughed as they all thought the kids had fallen asleep.

"You know guys, I was thinking the same thing," replied Bruce. "Let's keep reading and see what is next."

Everyone was fully awake now.

~BEVERLY'S JOURNAL~

Ninth Entry
Landings of the Starships

With the landing of the Starships our lives on Earth were totally different. The first thing that happened was that the News began to really be NEW. By that I mean that it was no longer the same old stories of wars and problems with money and people finally standing up for themselves.

For the first time in my life, people were talking about the future instead of the past. The Friends, which is the name we all called the Galactics, appeared on the Internet news, radio and television many times every day. Oh, yes, the word ET was replaced with the term Galactics.

One of first the things the Galactics told us was that they were not just our "Friends," they were also our family, our Galactic Family. You would think this would be shocking news, but everyone took it as if they already knew. Do you remember how I said before that the Ships somehow changed us, even before they landed?

I think that they opened our minds in some way. Well, actually, I know now that they did open our minds, and I know exactly how. What the Galactics did is that they "cut off" the constant stream of ELF waves (extremely low frequency waves) that were being broadcast through our airways via every possible means. These ELF waves were sent by the elite few who were actually running our world.

These ELF waves can have a huge effect on human behavior. With the external transmissions ended, we all began to remember and know things that we had never even thought of before. The Friends told us that without the external noise to mask our own inner states of consciousness, we would begin to download and integrate our multidimensional consciousness.

Our Galactic Friends also told us that while external forces were unconsciously controlling us, our inner Portal to the fifth dimension was beyond our conception. As usual, they were right about this. Shortly after they discontinued the transmission of these waves, we all began to have dreams and meditations of a great Portal opening before us.

In fact, we had these dreams and meditations so many times that when we saw the Portals in our daily consciousness, we were excited rather than frightened. Again, the Friends prepared us for changes in our third-dimensional reality by coming into our higher states of consciousness to assist us to "accept the impossible."

In fact, "accept the impossible" became our theme. So many things were changing in such sudden and impossible ways that we would have been reeling in confusion and anxiety if not for the Friends' teachings.

There is much more I would like to tell you about the ELF frequencies and Portals, but I must close for now. Besides, I don't know if you will be able to understand what I am talking about before you have gone through the Violet Light.

Tenth Entry

Lucid Dreaming

Once the Friends turned off the controlling frequency waves, which we never knew were there, we were so surprised to experience an inner quiet. Gradually, our dream lives became increasingly lucid, and our meditations began to take us on group journeys. Of course, we did not know that we were having the same meditation until we talked to each other.

However, once we found that more than a few of us were having the same meditation, we began sharing our meditations on the Internet so that people all over the world could know whether or not they, too, were sharing that experience. That was when we found out that our dreams and meditations of being in the Corridor were exactly the same all over the world.

I realize now that I never told you how I started going into the Tunnel, which I later discovered was the Arcturian Corridor. I never told you that information because I could not remember. Just as we all forgot our higher life when we took on a physical body, most of us forgot much about our physical life once we came here to New Earth.

I mean, we remembered our physical life in that we returned to assist others, but I just realized through the process of writing this journey that there are many holes in my memory about how I actually got here. I think that remembering how I got here was an important reason why I felt a need to write this message and send it to your timeline.

Actually, that sounds like an ego reason, but I guess that I aim to be a type of teacher here. Therefore, I will start my teaching by telling those in your timeline how you, too, can get here. In other words, as I teach you, I also teach myself.

Therefore, I had to remember the detail of how I entered that first tunnel, which I now know was a Portal, before I could share it with you. Since New Earth resonates to the fifth dimension, there is no "time" as you experience it in your dimension.

Therefore, putting events into a sequential form is something that we quickly forget upon our arrival. We do not need that skill. Therefore, there is no reason to retain it. In fact, our consciousness is fully calibrated to perceive all reality in a multidimensional fashion.

That is why I can look into your timeline to see that you are nearing the opening of the First Portals. Of course, there are myriad Portals that will open because all these Portals are accessed from within each person.

Portals inside yourself may seem very confusing to those of you who still function third-dimensionally, but our "frequency of reality" is accessed by *logging-out of your 3D Holographic Reality* and *logging-in to your true Multidimensional SELF*. You will *log-out* of that Holographic Reality through the Portal that you will find with your own higher dimensional perceptions.

Some of you will see these Portals, some of you will feel them, some of you will hear them and some of you will only experience them while you are asleep. I realize now that I was in my fourth-dimensional dream body when I found my first "tunnel," as I called it. I had to be asleep because my life had not come across any information that would allow me to believe that it could be possible to enter a Portal into a higher dimension of reality.

I write this journal in hopes that someone will read it. Then some of you may be able to become aware of the True reality that you are NOW experiencing via your Multidimensional SELF. I remember how confusing that statement is to time-bound thinking, so please believe me when I say that a reality in the NOW is ALWAYS occurring.

It is the challenge of keeping your consciousness awake to the frequency of my timeless reality, while also maintaining your physical shell, that is creating the great fatigue that I perceive in the bodies of your timeline.

I know that what I am saying may be very confusing. However, it is your time-bound thinking that ties you to a reality that is coming into its completion. I can see the myriad possible realities that are converging and intersecting in your world, and I wonder which of you will choose which possible reality.

I guess what I want to tell you is, "Please contact the highest expression of your SELF that you can imagine and allow that version of your Multidimensional SELF to assist you to make those choices." This highest expression of your SELF resonates to the octave of the Violet Light.

Ultraviolet is the highest perceivable light on any octave/dimension of your physical reality. Hence, it is the resonance that will allow you to transmute your consciousness into the next dimension of reality. In fact, it is the resonance of Violet Light that will guide you to the opening of your Portal into the higher frequency expressions of reality.

By the "time" I had adapted to the Indigo Light of the Corridor, I knew I was ready to become a higher version of my SELF, but I did not know how. Therefore, I needed to re-enter the Corridor. In other words, I was ready to go inside of myself to enter the Corridor in a fully conscious manner to return Home to my Multidimensional SELF.

Eleventh Entry
Preparing for Transition

I return to you now because I can see how many of you are preparing yourselves for your great transition. It is through the Violet Light, the "fire" of transmutation, that this transition begins. Once I had decided that I was ready to BE this higher version of my SELF that I felt deep within me, I began to feel myriad changes in my physical body.

Many of us thought that we were "sick," but because of my conscious decision to return to my true SELF, I knew that my "sickness" was my body trying to catch up with my consciousness. That is when I began to hear the voice of the Arcturians in my daily life.

The voice first began during meditation, which I had fully embraced by then. Then, I began to have a certain feeling that is difficult to describe. I would have to say that the feeling was an intense urge to stop, close my eyes, take a deep breath with a long exhale and listen to my inner Self.

As soon as I would do that, I would feel my consciousness begin to expand. Then, I had the feeling that my body was only a small part of "me," and there were many other parts of me beyond the confines of my physical form. I say "beyond" rather than "outside," because all of my higher frequency experiences seemed to be arising from "inside" of me.

When I turned my eyes around, actually my eye—my Third Eye—to look inside, I could see the Corridor. Very often before this time I found myself IN the Corridor, but I could not remember how I had entered it.

Now, for the first time, I could see the inner light that led to the entry to the Corridor. That light, of course, was violet. At first the violet light was very small, as if the opening to the Corridor was far away. But, how could the Corridor be far away if it was inside of me? Could I have been that vast within my SELF? The voice inside then said, "YOU, our beloved, are more vast than you can imagine."

This time I heard the voice echoing from deep, deep inside of me, and as I put my attention onto it, the violet light became brighter. I asked for more inner instructions and heard, "Follow the FEEL of our voice and the glow of the violet light." Upon hearing these words my body began to shake, and I had to focus on deep breathing to calm myself and, especially, to stay conscious.

There was a part of me that wanted to leave. At the time, I did not understand that feeling, but now I know that that was the part of me that was totally ready for ascension. However, there were other parts of me that still held fear and attachment to my old life. Hence, a battle started to be waged within me.

The shaking within my body became faster and my breathing deeper, almost desperate. I was losing ALL control of the situation. It was as if I was in a runaway car with no breaks. However, at the same time, I would not have used the breaks even if they were there.

I was beginning to experience a euphoric feeling beyond anything I had ever known. I then heard, "Surrender to your feelings and release all resistance." At first, all I could do was to say to myself, "Surrender and Release." I said this over and over, more times than I could count.

My words made me feel more in control, which calmed the fear I had not realized I was feeling. Then, I pulled all the shaking into my Core and slowed my breath. At that moment I felt like a rocket ship that had just been launched. I knew that my body was perfectly still, but my consciousness, my Essence, was soaring beyond the speed of light into the unknown. AND, I was loving it!

Never had I experienced such freedom and glory. I had had myriad experiences in the Corridor before, but nothing was like this. I hoped that I was still breathing and wondered if I would ever return. But to *where* would I return? To *Who* would I return? And, *why* would I ever want to leave here?

"It is not your time—yet!" whispered the inner voice, and suddenly, it was over.

I was back sitting on my chair with the biggest smile my face could imagine. All I could think was, "WOW!" I looked around my room. It was the same. My chair was the same, my desk was the same, and when I looked out the window, the world looked the same.

However, I was NOT the same. I knew that what I had experienced was a "preview of coming attractions," and I was very antsy to see the "entire movie."

"The Path to Ascension is paved with patience," spoke my inner voice. Again, a smile filled my face.

~LISA & BRUCE~

Lisa, Bruce and Joan were speechless, and the room seemed to be filled with violet light. "Of course I am just imagining that," they all thought, but no one said it. No one talked. Bruce and Lisa each scooped up a sleeping child and delivered them to their beds and Joan silently picked up her teacup, put it into the kitchen sink and returned to her small apartment above the garage.

With the children tucked in, Bruce and Lisa crawled into their own bed and instantly fell asleep. Would they even remember what had happened that night? Could they believe it if they did remember it? I was not possible for a room to be filled with violet light, was it?

But no one asked that question. They fell instantly asleep and did not awaken until noon the next day. Obviously, it was too late for the children to go to school, so they called a "second Sunday," They all, including Joan, laid around the house in their pajamas and grabbed whatever food they found in the kitchen.

They wandered around the house half asleep and half awake. They did not realize that the "sleeping" part was their physical body and their "awake" self was their fifth-dimensional Lightbody. When it was time for dinner, they walked to the local restaurant and talked about nothing important.

It was as if they were suspended between two worlds, and they were not in either one of them. "How long can we exist like this?" they all asked, even the children, who were now more mature than most adults. Everyone had made an inner shift. Even Leslie and Sam, who had seemed to be sleeping while Bruce read, had greatly changed.

None of them asked any questions or brought up the events of the night before. They needed time to integrate what had occurred. The adults had all connected with their inner child and the children had connected with their inner adult.

They did not know how that happened, but they knew something amazing was about to occur. It was as if it were a wish that would not come true if they spoke of it. However, it was NOT a wish. I was a reality, and none of them would ever be the same again.

PART V

Chapter XIII
THE JOURNAL
~Beverly's Story ~

It was almost a month before the "family" returned to the Journal. They had all known that they needed to integrate and understand what was occurring within them. They had also known that they needed to "fix up this old house," as Sam had so wisely said. No one had said anything, but they all secretly believed that if they fixed up the house, somehow they would find Beverly.

The joint project of deep cleaning, painting, replacing wallpaper and worn out rugs, was a collective project. Lisa and Bruce were discovering that when they fully included Leslie and Sam in their decisions, they acted almost like adults.

The reality was that the light meditations had expanded the children's consciousness to the extent that, even though they still wore child-like bodies, inside they were more like adults than most adults.

Once the house was completed, they decided to continue reading the Journal together. They had left off reading how Bob had transmuted into a higher frequency of himself, and they had all had their own version of that same experience.

They were ready now to look through the "open doorway" that their higher state of consciousness afforded them. It turned out that Beverly had also had a similar experience. This time they asked Joan to read while Lisa and Bruce sat on the floor with Leslie and Sam.

~BEVERLY'S JOURNAL~

Dear Journal,

This is Beverly. I realize that I have not added any dates for many entries, which is because I have been losing all concept of time. Also, since I read Bob's last entry, I have completely changed, but I don't know how. I guess that sentence is confusing, but to me it makes perfect sense.

I mean, I don't fully understand who I am now, or exactly what has changed, but I do know that my consciousness is greatly expanded. In fact, I am beginning to remember abilities that were "normal" when I was on the Ship, but were gradually lost during my long years in a physical body.

Now that I am remembering my true self, everything is changing so quickly that I have not entered the changes in the Journal. Fortunately, I did scribble out some notes. Better yet, because this expanded version of my self has no time, there is no forgetting. Hence, I believe that I can write an accurate account of what has so greatly altered my life.

Except that I have not been altered into a "new" life. Instead, the multidimensional consciousness that I had before I took this form has been fully restored. I know that my dear daughter, who is the child of two galactic beings, will also be able to remember her multidimensional SELF. Since Bruce is also a "starseed," my amazing grandchildren will eventually remember who they really are as well.

Dear, beloved Lisa, I know that one day you will find this Journal and allow it to transform you and your wonderful family in the same way that it has transformed me. Perhaps then you will be able to forgive me, and your father, for abandoning you emotionally, mentally and physically.

I love you and your family VERY much and await the NOW of our reunion.

~LISA & BRUCE~

Joan stopped reading and looked into Lisa's eyes as she asked, "Are you alright, honey?"

"Thanks for asking, Mom," she replied. "Yes, I am fine. I am wonderful. I am blessed. Thank you, Mom, both Moms. Please continue reading."

"Alright, dear," said Joan as she returned to reading the journal.

~BEVERLY'S JOURNAL~

I will now attempt to share my process exactly as it occurred. I hope that by telling you, my beloved family, about my process that you can forget me for leaving you. I also hope that my story can assist you to join me in this wonderful new world. My transformation started with what may or may not have been a dream.

In this dream, I was in between the fourth-dimensional world of sleep and the third-dimensional world in which I thought I was awake. However, after my communications with Bob I was pretty sure that I was awakening to another world. In fact, I often saw that "other world," but only for a brief moment.

At first I saw a doorway opening in my Third Eye through which I saw another reality. I could not enter that world, yet, but I could see it just past an invisible threshold. But as soon as I saw the threshold, I would fall back into sleep, or maybe that was when I awoke to the physical.

I was here alone in the house. I had turned off all the phones and stopped the mail. I did not know why I did that, but I somehow knew that I just had to follow my inner directives. Yes, they were directives, as if some higher version of myself was giving me instructions.

Then, those directives would leave as quickly as they appeared. Did I cross some kind of threshold or wake up? I could not determine the answer to that question because I would forget everything as soon as I awoke. Then, gradually, as I went about my daily life, I would know that it was the NOW to meditate and see if I could cross the threshold again.

This cycle went on and on. Finally, one time that I entered my meditation I knew that if I tried to control my meditation, it would not work. Therefore, I would have to "let go" or my ego would try to control my meditation. It was then that I realized how lost to the third dimension I had become with my negative emotions and self-pity.

That day, that moment, in that meditation, I vowed to be the Master of my ego and allow my true, multidimensional self to take the reigns of my life. As that decision settled into my heart and mind, I returned into my meditation chair and took some long, deep breaths.

I surrendered to all the myriad feelings that arose without falling into judgment or fear. In fact, I focused on loving my SELF unconditionally. Slowly the unconditional love of myself seeped deep into my heart and mind. It was then that I began to go into an even higher state of consciousness.

Yes, there it was again, the opening doorway. This time I easily flowed across the threshold for I had surrendered to my own multidimensional self. At first, I could not see very clearly, as it took me a while to adapt to the higher frequencies of this reality.

As I relaxed into my experience, I remembered my SELF on the Ship and knew from my sensations that I was in the fifth dimension. But I was not on the Ship. In fact, I was pretty sure I was on fifth-dimensional New Earth.

I was still a bit out-of-sync with the higher resonance, so I could only vaguely perceive my surroundings, and I couldn't interact with them. It was as if I were a ghost. I could see many things, but my hand could not grasp them, nor could I get anyone's attention.

I took a long moment to breathe deeply and completely surrender to my process. I allowed all thoughts of "what I had left behind" to flow out of my awareness and focused my attention on this new reality. Actually, I sensed that this reality was not *new* because it felt familiar, yet different. Perhaps it was I who was different.

I knew that I had lived myriad incarnations in the third and fourth dimensions, but had not been able to remember any of my excursions into the fifth-dimensional realm. It was an agreement I made when I came here from the Starship to assist Gaia.

Don't ask me how I knew that, but it was part of the many things that I had somehow remembered, but did not know. As I relaxed into my SELF, I slowly remembered that I had come from several, yes several, galaxies. It seems that I was a "galactic hybrid" because my Oversoul had taken incarnations in many Galactic Worlds.

I remembered that David and I were amongst a group of galactic citizens who had volunteered to take a physical vessel to assist planet Earth. Once we arrived, we moved into different timelines and locations on Earth. We, who were the members of our group mission, saw that once again Gaia's visitors had almost destroyed Her planet.

When we first saw Gaia in Her fifth-dimensional expression we rejoiced, but when we landed on Earth's third-dimensional habitat zone, we were filled with sorrow. I had to return to this meditation again and again to release this sorrow. Then, I had to return to this meditation again and again to re-train my brain to recover the many memories that could not resonate to the brain of my third-dimensional earth vessel.

Slowly, as I continued the meditations of perceiving the opened doorway, I began to regain my innate feelings of freedom. This sensation of freedom made me feel as light as a feather and as expanded as a soaring Eagle. Reviewing my past also helped me to remember how to adapt to this higher frequency of reality.

Even when I was not meditating, I began to close my eyes for a long moment and focus on my breath. I would then place my hands on my Heart and feel how the higher resonance of the reality through the "Doorway" filled me with the peace and calm.

Eventually, I began to feel the sensation of unconditional love. This unconditional love was not based on what I did or did not know, do or desire. The feeling of unconditional love embraced me and healed me of all that had held me back.

Gradually, this unconditional love moved into the circuitry of my physical eyes, so that I could better perceive this world through my Third Eye. At first, my Third Eye could only see straight ahead of me. But as I continued to practice looking through my Third Eye the range of my inner vision expanded, and I could clearly see in all directions.

At first, my human brain was straining to see in all directions at once, so I stopped all inner intention of sharing my experience with my physical self. Then, one day I could "feel" my ego-self asking me to share my experience.

As I shared my expanded vision with my ego-self, I could feel my multidimensional self expand into the fifth-dimensional frequencies of perception. It was then that I perceived the fifth-dimensional reality of New Earth. My conscious perception of New Earth allowed me to remember my Mission.

We, the members of my away team to transmuting Earth, took a physical body to remember how many lives ago we too had lived on a planet on the cusp of ascension. Fortunately, I remained grounded in my physical self so that I could bi-locate to fifth-dimensional New Earth while I remained fully grounded on third/fourth-dimensional Earth. In other words, I was able to be aware and grounded in third-dimensional Earth while I simultaneously experienced fifth-dimensional New Earth.

I was ONE with my third-dimensional self, while I was also ONE with my fifth-dimensional SELF to whom I was bi-locating. In other words, I was on the higher dimensions of New Earth, but I was also sitting in a chair on third-dimensional Earth.

When I thought of my physical self through this expanded perspective, I could feel the challenges that I confronted. In order to consciously bi-locate, I had to embrace a greater detachment from the many challenges of physical Earth. At the same time, I had had to create a deeper bond to Earth and my loved ones.

I had finally accomplished the reunion with my own higher self, but I had not yet reunited with my physical family. Then I remembered that Earth was becoming New Earth, while New Earth already existed in the higher dimensions. Only within the timeless NOW of the fifth dimension to which I was finally returning could I understand that fact.

When I first came to Earth, I had to adapt to the density of my physical body, whereas my form on New Earth was of a finer, higher frequency with wavering boundaries and flowing shapes. If I could merge my higher frequency self with my physical frequency self, perhaps I could assist other humans to do the same.

Then, if each of those persons merged with Gaia's third-dimensional planet, and transmuted back to the resonance of fifth-dimensional Earth, perhaps they could assist Gaia to do the same. However, it was clear that it would take many humans bonded in unity to do that, and I had not even bonded with my own family.

How did I go so wrong? How did I forget to love my daughter, her family, my house and my friends? How did I get so lost in the illusions of the third dimension that I forgot why I came here in the first place?

~LISA & BRUCE~

"THAT IS IT!" Bruce shouted as he stood up. "That is exactly what we will teach at our Center! We can teach people how to bond with their higher self so that they can use that unified consciousness to bond with the planet. Once bonded with the planet, they could work with their own higher self to assist the planet."

"And I can teach kids that they actually know more than their parents," laughed Sam.

"I will teach them to sing from their hearts," said Leslie.

"And I will teach the seniors that they are never too old to be creative or to start a new life," said Joan.

But, Lisa was quiet.

"What about you, honey?" asked Bruce. It was only then that he actually looked at her.
"What is wrong, Lisa?"

It took Lisa a while to discover what was wrong with her, but she knew that it was something about her mother. Everyone waited patiently while she figured it out.

"Mom said she hadn't even bonded with her own family," she finally said, trying not to cry again.

"Well," said Sam. "We will find her and make her bond with us."

Everyone, except for Lisa, laughed. Then Sam got up and walked over to her and said, "If I lost you, Mom, I would not stop looking until I found you. So we will do the same for Grandma."

Now Lisa was crying as she pulled Sam into her arms. "Yes, my brave and wonderful son. We WILL look until we find her."

"Yes," echoed Bruce, as he put his arm around her. Leslie got up to join the family hug and said, "We will find her, Mommy, I feel it in my heart."

Joan watched from across the room and softly said, "I feel it in my heart, too."

After that emotional moment, they all got up and went into the kitchen to fix a meal.

When the family returned for the next reading of the Journal, it was Bob who had written again. This time Lisa asked to read, maybe to distract herself from too many emotions.

~BEVERLY'S JOURNAL~

Dear Journal,

I am writing a bit out of sequence in that I have already received these messages from Bob on New Earth. I am explaining what occurred in the hopes that my daughter finds this Journal and is reading it. You can see below that I wrote, "If there is any more information from Bob, I am happy to document it."

However, before I had a chance to type the answer in my computer, the answer just appeared as if someone else was using my keyboard. By this point, there is nothing that shocks me, so I just watched as Bob gave his explanation below:

First Message
Bob's Inter-dimensional Computer

Dear Beverly,

I am Bob, communicating with you by writing directly into your computer. I am happy to continue my messages to you. I wish to thank you for sharing my information with others. Group consciousness is very important to assist Gaia's transmutation into the higher dimensions of Her planetary self.

As I may have said, I would be perceived via your third-dimensional perception as a young man. However, young and old are third-dimensional terms, as we do not age in the fifth dimension. But, that is not the topic that I wanted to share with you today. In your today, as I experience no time on New Earth, I wish to speak about the importance of unity consciousness.

It is great to see how our timelines have intermingled. I wonder if that is why I felt I had to write directly into your journal. Maybe I was just listening to that *Inner Voice* of the Friends. I wonder what will happen when our timelines completely merge.

Will we return to ONE world again, or will we still remain one of the myriad versions of Earth flowing through the essence of multidimensional realities? You see there are many versions of Earth, some fully ascended, such as mine, and some newly ascending.

Your reality, Beverly, is on the verge of arrival in our reality.

In fact, I see that you are visiting us, but your third-dimensional consciousness cannot remember your visits because you can't interact with us yet. Once you begin to interact with us, it will be easier for you to remember your fifth-dimensional excursions to New Earth.

I can see that you, for we are all fully telepathic here, are wondering how I can answer your questions via writing into your computer. As you may have guessed, we use quantum, biological computers, QBC's, to write in our journals. Since we are all ONE here, everything we write in our journals is automatically shared with everyone.

Because our computers are biological, they have consciousness. In fact, they all function via a unified consciousness. Therefore, when anyone makes an entry in any of our QBCs, their message is automatically entered into ALL the QBCs. Furthermore, because they are quantum, they are not time-bound. These QBC computers are extremely cool.

We can ask any question we want, and the answer will instantly appear. This process is much like typing a question into your 3D search engine and choosing from the many possible answers. I say possible answers because different types of realities would have their own answers for the same question.

Oh, there is another new arrival. This person is almost able to stabilize her frequency rate to our resonance. I am going to log off for a moment and see if I can be of assistance. Oh, I hope I did not frighten you by writing directly into your computer. You see, you and I have become inter-dimensionally bonded. Therefore I can write directly into your computer.

~LISA & BRUCE'S FAMILY~

"Cool," exclaimed Sam. "I wonder if Bob would write into our computer?"

"That is a great question," said Bruce. "I think we would need to write to Bob and see if we can establish an inter-dimensional relationship with him, like Beverly did."

"I don't know," said Lisa. "I think this concept is even too weird for me."

"But it is not too weird for Sam, and he is likely the generation that will be having these experiences," responded Bruce.

"It is not too weird for me either," said Leslie. "Can I bond with Bob, too?"

"Another good question. Let's let Mom keep reading and see if we can find any answers," said Bruce.

~BEVERLY'S JOURNAL~

Second Message
Just Let GO

Hello again. Bob here. Sorry I had to log-off. We have an agreement here that whenever a new being appears, we stop what we are doing to offer assistance. I say "being" rather than "person" because non-human life forms are also entering this higher frequency of Earth.

In fact, many of the animals and plants that have become "extinct" on Matrix Earth are alive and well on New Earth. Since all life here is conscious and able to communicate with other life forms, we are able to assist plants, animals and elementals, as well as humans.

It is a wonderful experience for us to be able to communicate with animals, plants and the Sylphs (air elementals), Undines (water elementals), Gnomes (earth elementals) and Salamanders (fire elementals). These wonderful beings do not speak English, as I am doing now, but neither do we.

On New Earth all life speaks a language that is free of time and space. It is the language that humans, plants, animals, and elementals have always spoken. Hence, we are quite amazed and pleased that we can communicate with them. It is also an experience for us, especially the new humans who have always felt separate from Mother Nature, to commune with all the plants, animals, and elementals.

On the other hand, learning this manner of communication, which we call Light Language, is one of the biggest challenges for the New Ones. They try to move their tongues and express separate words in a linear fashion.

This manner of communication is appropriate for a reality based on the separation and linear thinking that comes from time. However, that means of communication does not work in a reality which resonates to the HERE and NOW.

Communication on New Earth is a form of communing with each other by merging our consciousness. In this manner, pictures, emotions, and thought-forms are automatically transferred to each other, as well as into the group consciousness.

In fact, whenever there is a new arrival to New Earth, their entire history of incarnations in duality is instantly copied to the crystalline field that contains our world. This information also goes into the Quantum Biological Computers that we can all access.

When we first come here, we usually access the QBC via an interface within our living quarters. However, as we adapt to our new life, we realize that we can simply direct our thoughts into the Group

Consciousness of the crystalline field and all answers will be instantly available.

Since New Earth serves as an interface between the third/fourth dimension and the mid-fifth dimension, there are many communication "devices" or "machines" for the "new arrivals" to use until they become comfortable with the myriad multidimensional powers that we all have within our group consciousness.

Learning our forms of communication is actually the second challenge that our new arrivals have when they enter our world. Their first challenge is to totally master their every thought and emotion so that they can stay here. Do you remember that I said that I often assisted the new arrivals from Matrix Earth when I first arrived?

My assignment was to assist those who could not master their thoughts and emotions. I was given this task because when I first arrived I was frightened and released fearful thoughts and emotions from my aura. These fearful thoughts and emotions instantly lowered my resonance and I "fell out" of this reality.

It is a very emotional experience to enter an entirely different frequency of reality. Therefore, even after I released my fear, I would "fall out," as we call it, because my excitement quickly fell into agitation. This agitation also made me "fall out."

Eventually, I learned to hold a calm and loving acceptance, which was almost like *no* thoughts and *no* emotions. This centered state of consciousness allowed me to release my 3D concepts of space, time, possible, and impossible. With this release, I could "fall into" the *here* and *now* of my experience. Because I have found a way to master my fear-based thoughts and emotions, I was assigned to assist the new arrivals with that challenge.

Since the new arrivals come here with the habit of separation, so many different forms of life often frighten them. Furthermore, many are new to the concept of thought transference and believed that they could not communicate with different forms of beings.

Fortunately, I crossed over with a group of people. Then, as soon as I saw them, we hugged, exchanged stories, and listened to each other's experiences of mastering our fearful thoughts and emotions. With the support of my friends, I was able to maintain my self-mastery and was able to stay here on New Earth.

Another challenge for the new arrivals is the discovery that ALL their thoughts and emotions are shared with the unity consciousness of our world. This realization often frightens the new ones, which lowers their consciousness back to the third/fourth dimension and they fall out.

Because of this situation, many of us are using whatever means we can imagine to teach possible new ones while they are still in the third dimension. It is for this reason that I am writing directly into your computer. We know that education and love are the best ways to heal fear.

Therefore, we have many individual and group meditations that we send to those who are preparing themselves to log-out of the 3D matrix. An "individual meditation" is when the 3D one's body is alone, but they are still able to tune into our fifth-dimensional Group Mind.

A "group meditation" is when a group of people in the third dimension merge into a unified group to receive a message from our fifth-dimensional Group Mind. You see, our Group Mind serves as an open window or portal into the lower octaves of the fifth dimension.

Often awakening ones can only perceive the "half-way" mark where they can still maintain many concepts, traditions, and habits from their many sojourns into the third/fourth dimension. In this manner, their adaptation to a totally different concept of life can be gradual.

Many of us greatly enjoy the first, *transitional stage* of New Earth. In this lowest sub-plane of the fifth dimension, all that we have wished for in our third-dimensional reality is instantly experienced. There can be great healing and contentment within this transmutation energy field.

When the new arrivals are ready to move on to the next sub-plane of New Earth, they will no longer have the experiences of separation or limitation that still occurs within the transitional stage of the first sub-plane. From here on we *never* perceive a line, or threshold, which divides New Earth from 3D Matrix Earth.

From our fifth-dimensional point of view, we are in the process of a gradual, or swift, alteration in our thoughts, feelings, states of consciousness, perceptions, and creative force. Our adjustment to this reality is an ongoing adventure filled with unconditional love, unity consciousness, and inter-dimensional adventures.

Dear Beverly, we welcome you to join our adventure. Just "let go" and surrender to the love and light that is filling your world. We can see you, and, soon, you will see us.

~THE FAMILY~

"I feel like we are getting very close to something," said Lisa to her family unit of Bruce, Leslie, Sam and Joan. "It seems that the next message continues with a similar message. Is it fine with you all if I continue reading?"

Everyone agreed, so Lisa read the next section.

~BEVERLY'S JOURNAL~

Third Entry
Protecting the Embryo of New Earth

Hello Beverly. I am Bob, returned via my QBC to speak to you via my ever expanding Group Mind of New Earth. I am wondering how long I will maintain a sense of the "me" who was once known as Bob. Therefore, the Group Mind wanted me to tell you about protecting the embryo of New Earth.

We want you to know that inside of each of you is the embryo of New Earth. Since all of you are ONE within your Multidimensional SELF, all of you are ONE with New Earth. Thus, all ascending ones have within them a personal expression of their experience of New Earth.

Some of you are awakening to this "you," but others are not yet resonating to a frequency in which they can hold that frequency of consciousness. Either way, there is a new and unique feeling within you that you never dared express before now. We observe that the ones who will be joining us on New Earth have protected this embryo of New Earth. Many of you have even consciously expanded it.

Because your outer world (your life in the 3D Game) is still filled with fear, danger and hard work, you could not feel this embryo until NOW. Before you were so busy facing the many challenges of survival on the physical plane that you had *no time* to look within.

In fact, even if you did look within, you could not perceive this "embryo" because your Higher SELF had placed it in an inter-dimensional capsule to protect it. But now that the frequency of Gaia is constantly rising, your multidimensional consciousness is continuously expanding, and many of you are having glimpses of this embryo.

Dear Beverly, we ask you to take a moment to feel this new sensation deep within your core. Imagine a small embryo, wound up like a Mobius coil, slowly and steadily growing within your High Heart. You have carried this embryo within your Three Fold Flame in every incarnation, but the frequency of Earth was usually too low for the embryo to start the process of re-birth.

Beverly, we ask that you allow yourself to FEEL the inner sweetness that can only arise from innocence and purity. Feed this embryo with your own expanding unconditional love and multidimensional light.

FEEL this delicate new place within you and protect it with your life. Notice the food that allows this embryo to grow and the food that can cause it pain. Tune into this virgin place within you that has never been tarnished by the harshness and stress of daily life.

FEEL how this delicacy and inner promise allows you to identify any thoughts, emotions, people, places and/or things that make you forget your New SELF. Turn around inside yourself and look directly into this embryo.

Allow this immense sweetness and ancient wisdom to flow into your consciousness. Remember times in your life when you experienced a whisper of this presence, but you forgot how to make it "work" in daily life.

As you look into this embryo of your fifth-dimensional SELF, vow to protect it from that which lowers your consciousness and makes you forget the YOU that you are becoming. Determine to create the life in which your embryo can move out of its cocoon and fill your present form with your multidimensional memory.

Feed this embryo of unconditional love by making choices that allow you to have time to nurture your emerging SELF. As you go about your day, remember to caress your High Heart and send a brief message of recognition to your fifth-dimensional embryo.

This growing expression of your SELF is your passport to New Earth. New Earth is not a place. New Earth is a frequency. You will "become" New Earth as you raise the frequency of your third-dimensional thinking into the steady flow of multidimensional thinking and transmute your emotional responses to unconditional love.

As you go about your daily life, remember to ask, "How will my New SELF respond to this situation?" Become aware of the areas of your life that feed your growing experience of Being and release that which drags you into the mire of drudgery and forgetfulness.

In this manner, you will create a life filled with the sweetness, love, creativity, and adventure in which your New SELF can thrive. See this *new* you in the eyes of your children, your mate, your best friends, your colleagues at work, the faces that pass you on the street and the checker at the grocery store.

Most of all see your New SELF in the mirror as you look into your eyes and say,

"I AM becoming my New SELF!"

~THE FAMILY~

Everyone in the room, even the children, were totally quiet and remained as still as a stone. Finally Lisa whispered, "She is there. Mom is on New Earth. I just KNOW it!"

Chapter XIV
THE JOURNAL
~Beverly's Transition ~

~BEVERLY'S JOURNAL~

Dear Journal,

It has been a while since I heard from Bob. Since I have not been putting the dates into my Journal entries, or working, or seeing anyone, or even leaving the house except to get food, I seem to have lost all sense of time. I am not sure if I am resonating to the higher dimensional consciousness that I had when I first entered this 3D body, or if I am "going crazy," as they say in the physical world.

No, I know I am not going crazy. That was just my feeling alone and lonely. It is said that the darkest night is just before dawn, so maybe I am right on schedule. I have been writing my life in this Journal for a long time now, and I thought I was beginning to remember how to return Home to my true SELF on the Ship or on New Earth.

The other day I think I even saw my friend Bob in my meditation. I could see him coming towards me, but just as he reached out to take my hand, he disappeared. Actually, he stayed where he was, and I disappeared from his reality. I took that vision as a message that, if I do return to my Ship, it will be via New Earth.

Something about that vision made me get busy or lazy, and I fell into my ego. Whatever happened, that moment ended and I could no longer communicate with Bob. Finally I realized that, once again, I was trying to escape this reality, which lowered my consciousness so much that I lost my higher perceptions.

I decided that I would have to go back to take a deep look at my life before I could move forward. Therefore, I finally pulled together all the messages that I have gotten since 1995 and put them into a Journal. I left a message for Lisa, just in case she comes here and finds this Journal.

I made a lot of mistakes in my life, but I also had the love of a good husband and a sweet daughter. After both of them left my life I fell into depression for many years. However, I finally pulled myself out of my own self-pity and started to help others.

As I increasingly found ways to help others, my life took on more meaning. I finally came to peace with my life and realized that I did contribute to others and to the planet. I hope that Lisa finds and reads this Journal. I have not given her anything in many years, but I learned a great deal through talking with my higher dimensional friends.

Their words have brought me peace and purpose, and I hope they do the same for Lisa. I came here from my Starship, but I understand now that my next mission is to go to the New Earth to assist in the same manner as Bob. Of course, the correct word is not "going" to New Earth as New Earth is not a place. New Earth is a frequency.

Therefore, to experience New Earth, I have been meditating to calibrate my consciousness to that frequency. I have discovered that returning to that frequency is not too difficult. What is challenging is maintaining that consciousness while the remnants of my 3D brain are saying, "This is impossible. I can't just go to New Earth by changing my consciousness."

Then, of course, those doubts lower my consciousness, and I have yet another failed attempt. Not that I have made too many attempts. I have been avoiding my fear of failure by being "busy" doing other "really important" things. But how could anything be more important than experiencing New Earth?

I think that that is a question that I must answer with complete honesty. So here goes... How could anything be more important than experiencing New Earth? To be totally honest, I will have to allow this question to settle into my heart and mind for there is no easy answer.

I guess I can begin with the first thing that comes into my mind, which is, "I am not quite ready." But, then, I realize that I AM ready. So why am I waiting? Yes, I must admit that I would love to see Lisa and her family at least one time before I leave. I need to apologize in person for all the times that I was unable to participate in her life in the way that she needed.

Also, I feel as though there is something more that I need to do in my physical reality. I want to experience the "shift." I have waited and planned for this "NOW" for decades. Therefore, since I have waited this long, I can wait a bit longer. I don't want to miss anything.

I want to experience the conclusion of the "movie" from front row seat. Will NESARA actually happen? If so, how will it feel to be FREE of all debt for the rest of reality? Will the Galactics actually land? If so, how will our world respond?

Can I really experience my reality on New Earth as deeply as I am experiencing the reality in which I am writing this entry? I don't want to jump to the ending. I want to experience every word, every day, every event with my mind clear and my heart open.

Or, maybe I am making excuses because I don't want to leave my people, my home, and my life. Am I afraid? I must ask myself this. No, I don't feel at all afraid now. However, if a Starship lands in my front yard, will I be afraid, or will I be joyous. I want to wait and see.

I want to experience the fulfillment of what I have spent my life dreaming about. I have to think some more, as the real answers to my question are very deep. Be back later.

****

Dear Journal,

While I was away "thinking" I remembered that I was thinking in a third-dimensional manner. I was thinking as though I could only have one reality at a time. In fact, I was thinking as though time, as I know it here, is the same in every dimension.

I know that that is not true, but the habit of my third-dimensional thinking was triggered by my emotions of thinking that I had to make a choice and had to "give up" something to get something. In other words, I was thinking from my time-bound ego and not from my timeless Multidimensional SELF.

I can see that third-dimensional habits are not easily released. What other third-dimensional habits do I need to release to be able to consciously experience New Earth? I know that my mundane mind will not be able to answer that question.

I also know that my Multidimensional Mind can instantly give me the answer. Therefore, all I need do is to call upon my Multidimensional SELF. Up until now, I would "channel" the information by asking the Journal to connect me with the higher dimensional beings.

But, I have now come to accept that many of those Beings are a component of my SELF. I also realize that those higher beings are also a component of everyone who holds a form on 3D Earth. Hence, I am endeavoring to find a way to perceive my "Guides," such as the Arcturians, not as Beings above me, but as Beings inside of me.

I have been trying to release the polarized thinking about sequential realities aligned in a hierarchical fashion, with myself in the lowest realm. I know that my true self is multidimensional and that in the higher frequencies of reality there are NO illusions of time.

With that illusion of time released, I can release the feeling of separation and limitation that time creates. Therefore, instead of calling "up" to my Guide, I am endeavoring to expand my consciousness to encompass that embryo of my SELF that resonates "within."

I will begin by calling upon the ME that resonates to New Earth. I know that this exercise can be more difficult than I think. Therefore, I am asking my time-bound ego to merge with an expression of my multidimensional SELF who can believe that it is my chosen mission to join New Earth.

Furthermore, I ask my third-dimensional mind to "take a rest." I am thankful for my 3D brain, as it got me this far. It will *not* become obsolete because my multidimensional self will be communicating with humans for as long as necessary. I don't really know what that statement means, but I am willing to adjust to living in the unknown.

I think I can make that adjustment because I have a feeling that the unknown will be joyful and filled with love. In fact, the present is pretty good too. I also know that I can let go of a lot of the aspects in my physical life, in fact, I already have.

Now, I am now ready to converse with a higher expression of my SELF. I allow my heart and mind to open and commune with the Flow of a higher expression of my SELF…

"Hello, I AM the ONE who resonates to New Earth. I know, and remember when, I/we were in the timeline of the last years before transitioning to New Earth. It is not that that transition has already occurred and you missed it. The transition has occurred.

"However, it occurred beyond time, so you, my time-bound ego, are having difficulty understanding that concept. Therefore, I will call on my fifth-dimensional SELF and your ego-self to also remain grounded in your third-dimensional transitional reality.

"Dear version of my SELF on New Earth," my 3D self calls. (By now I am not quite sure who I am.)

"Yes," I hear a distant response, "I am the you on New Earth."

Obviously I am still in the third dimension as it takes some *time* for me to receive the response.

"Dear Self on New Earth, can you assist me with my the transition from physical Earth to New Earth? Is the transition different with everyone, or is there a process that applies to everyone?"

"Yes," I hear a higher dimensional expression of my SELF say. "There is a constant process, which intermingles and flows freely into and out of the many versions of New Earth and physical Earth.

"There is no sequence, and the best word in your vocabulary to explain this process would be the word 'practice.' When you first learn a new language, you need to practice speaking it if you wish to retain your new skill.

"When you first have experiences of New Earth, please practice returning to the physical, then to New Earth, then physical Earth, again-and-again. By moving back and forth between these dimensions, you will no longer *be* the person that you were when you first visited New Earth.

"You see, your entire biochemistry and neural circuitry changes every time you make this shift. Therefore, it is very important that you calibrate your consciousness to both frequencies of reality.

"In this manner, YOU are conscious of the fact that YOU are choosing to change your life by creating a new YOU. You will not be 'time traveling,' as the location of New Earth has NO time. Instead, you are learning to Flow within the ONE.

"When you choose to be ONE with the Flow, you are choosing to allow yourself to enter the process of transmuting your third-dimensional, physical body into your fifth-dimensional, Light-body. If you choose to maintain an open portal with New Earth, even for a few of your seconds, a ripple of creative change moves through your entire world.

"This change occurs because you are actually creating inter-dimensional portals through which we can send the fifth-dimensional frequency of New Earth into the actual body of Gaia's third-dimensional planet.

"Because of Gaia's Law of Free Will, a member of your reality must choose to open a portal from your frequency into our frequency. Then, we can respond to your free-will choice by sending a massive burst of higher frequency energy into Gaia's physical form.

"This burst of multidimensional light and unconditional love ripples through all third-dimensional worlds. However, many of the third-dimensional ones may only experience the fourth-dimensional octaves of our energetic gift because they are not yet ready to accept fifth-dimensional energy fields.

"Fortunately, many of you are accustomed to perceiving the fourth dimension because that is the frequency of your dreams. Hence, even though you may not be aware of it, your brief venture into New Earth has created a huge impact in your third-dimensional life.

"Because of your continuous efforts, you are beginning to understand what is occurring via your dreams. Hence, we ask you to continue visiting us. We are here and clearly see you even if you do not see us. Meditate as often as you can to continually expand you consciousness. Your meditations will also assist you to download and activate your innate multidimensional thinking.

"We perceive that many of you are having dreams that are guiding you into your transition. Since fourth-dimensional time is faster than your 3D time, these fourth-dimensional experiences of your dream body are greatly assisting you to release your addiction to time.

"Your great adventure is beginning, Beverly. Have fun."

~THE FAMILY~

Everyone, even the children, was quiet after that message. They all sat in silence for what seemed to be the no-time of the fifth dimension. Perhaps it was.

Then Bruce realized how late it was and announced that it was time for bed.

Everyone slowly got up to go silently to bed, even the children who always complained. The answer to that anomaly came when Bruce heard Sam softly say to Leslie, "Do you want to meet on New Earth again tonight?"

Bruce knew that he would have another sleepless night. Maybe he couldn't sleep because he was afraid of what seemed to be occurring in his dreams. In their next family reading of the Journal, he got the answers he needed.

This time, it was Bruce who read the Journal for everyone to hear.

~BEVERLY'S JOURNAL~

Dear Journal,

The last two nights I have been saying before I go to sleep, "I want to go to New Earth tonight and remember my experience." I did *not* remember my experiences when I woke up, but during the next day I found new concepts in my mind that were not there before.

For example, yesterday while I was obsessively thinking about how I wanted to have a physical feeling of New Earth, I realized that it would not be possible. Again, I was thinking third-dimensionally about how we experience life in the higher dimensions.

I have been learning from Bob that the experience of life in a reality based on separation and density is very different from the experience of reality based on unity consciousness and high frequency Flow of the fifth dimension. It was then that I realized that the sensation of touch would be very different in the fifth dimension. For example, when we touch something in the third dimension, our separate, physical hand meets a separate person, animal, plant, or object.

Therefore, when we have the experience of touching an object, we feel only the surface of that object. Also, if we touch another person or animal we feel only the surface of that being. On the other hand, in the fifth dimension we are not separate. We all extend our auras beyond the form that we are currently using.

An aura has an emanation that expands and contracts. Consequently, there are *not* two clearly defined surfaces that interact via physical touch. Instead, there are two auras that merge and flow into each other, as an aura does not have a surface.

Furthermore, in the higher frequency realities we are the conscious creators of every "thing." First we consciously chose our thoughts. We then fill those thoughts with emotions to create "thought forms." These thought forms carry our *every* thought and emotion into *every* interaction that we have with *every* life form.

Hence, our experience of touch is not surface against surface but emanation merging into emanation. In fact, all of New Earth and beyond is based on emanations merging and interacting within the Flow of the multiple possibilities flowing from *every* emanation.

These possibilities shift and change with our every thought and emotion. Also, in the fifth dimension and beyond, the polarities of fear/love, you/me, good/bad, etc., do not exist. Most important, our ego "shell" no longer exists to create and perceive these polarities.

Without the third-dimensional thinking of our ego, the cumbersome nature of a hierarchical system based on separation, comparison, competition and desire for what we "don't have" no longer exists. These limiting concepts are replaced with, and healed by, our Multidimensional SELF.

"Hello," Bob writes via his QBC directly into my computer. "I see that you are beginning to remember your visits to New Earth while in your human consciousness. Congratulations."

"Oh, hi," I type into my computer. "Yes, I am beginning to remember. I think I even remember you. Were you the one last night that was reminding me about my Multidimensional Self? Could you please write that answer into my computer so my family can see when they read my Journal?"

~THE FAMILY~

"Does she know we are reading her Journal?" everyone said at once.

Then they all laughed. There had been so much laughter in the house lately. Joan had even found a boyfriend who often joined them for meals. Also, Leslie and Sam often had friends over to play on the cool swing set, trampoline and climbing apparatus. Bruce, with help from both kids, had even made a fort in the old tree at the back of their backyard.

Bruce and Lisa were using the office four days a week, with special seminars once a month. Also, Bruce had discovered that he had a healing touch. When Sam jumped out of the swing set and hit his head, Bruce instinctive touched the bleeding wound. Instantly, the bleeding stopped and the injury was gone.

They decided to keep that event a family secret. They knew that change was difficult for people, but it had gradually become natural for them. Bruce and Lisa knew that their children were "starseeds," just as Beverly had said what seemed like a lifetime ago.

In fact, they were all remembering other lifetimes, and were very interested when they read Bob's next entry.

~BEVERLY'S LAST ENTRY~

Dear Journal,

Today I had the most amazing experience. I actually saw the Arcturian in my room, just in front of the door, the portal, the entrance and the exit. I could feel, see and accept the perception of the Arcturian coming towards me and standing directly in front of me.

"Would you like to go to New Earth?" I heard the Arcturian whisper into my heart.

"Oh yes, so very yes," I answered.

I could actually feel the Arcturian smiling, so I guess my effusiveness was all right.

Of course the Arcturian heard my thoughts and said, "The 'effusiveness' as you say, is the energy field that is necessary for you to make this journey. Now you must build a thought form, which is your personal inter-dimensional portal."

"How do I do that?" I asked.

"We will, of course, assist you. Begin by moving into the frequency of NO thoughts. What that means is that you allow your third-dimensional brain to release all influence over your thought process." After waiting, the Arcturian continued. "Good. Do you feel how something is shifting within you?"

"Yes, yes, I do feel the shift," I replied. "In fact, I feel that my old fears from my experiences of abduction by the Zetas have been released and have greatly shifted. I once thought of my abduction as a fearful event, but I now realize that I had volunteered to share my DNA with them. They then implanted my old fear of spaceships in my mind as a tool to help me find and release my deepest third-dimensional fears.

"I can even remember how the Zetas had me and the other children sit under what they called 'The Learning Tree.' I now realize that the implanted fear of my experiences with the Zetas made me forget all the wonderful learnings that entered my mind and heart when I sat before the Learning Tree. This is all so very exciting."

"Do not allow excitement to lower your frequency. This is not a joy ride at an amusement park. This is the final destination after more incarnations than you could remember. You are about to take a journey that you will create with your multidimensional mind, your Third Eye and your High Heart.

"Relax and allow your third-dimensional brain to release its hold on your consciousness. Do you see how old judgments and fears are coming to the surface of your awareness so that you can release them?"

"Yes, I do," I responded.

"Please send unconditional love to all these fears and judgments. In this manner you can extract them from the matrix of your third-dimensional brain. Now use the Violet Fire to transmute them into their higher frequencies of love and light."

It took me a while to seek out all the fearful and judgmental thoughts that I needed to unconditionally love free. Fortunately, these old thought forms from many third-dimensional lives seemed to wait patiently within my aura. It was almost as if these thought forms knew that they would be transmuted into a higher frequency by the Violet Fire.

"We see that you are observing how your thoughts are active, alive beings," said the Arcturian.

"Yes," I said/thought, as this was a telepathic conversation. "Thank you for explaining what was happening. I never realized that thoughts were alive."

"Yes," responded the Arcturian. "But do not get distracted, please continue with your process."

The Arcturian was correct, as I did distract myself by thinking about what I was thinking about. No, it was the self-judgment of my thoughts that distracted me. Therefore, I decided to release all self-judgment and give myself a pat on the back for being able to experience this NOW.

"Wonderful idea," I heard the Arcturian say. "You are allowing your thoughts to reveal to you the type of thought forms each thought is creating."

"Thank you," I said. "With your assistance, I am realizing that now. I will try to calm myself by loving my self unconditionally."

"Good idea," replied the Arcturian.

I chanted over and over, "I love my self unconditionally. I love my self unconditionally." Finally, I started to believe it. I actually began to love my self without condition.

That is when it started. By holding the thought of unconditional love within my heart, as well as sending it through my body, I began to actually perceive the thought form of unconditional love for my self. The thought form was a pearly, pink light that glowed with the healing energies of unconditional love.

At first the sensation of actually loving myself unconditionally was so overwhelming that I began to sob. However, my crying was not from sadness. I cried from release, relief, and the pure joy of being my true self.

"Did I really hold that much hostility towards my own self?" I asked.

"Yes," answered the Arcturian. "How does it feel to release it?"

"It feels like euphoria. It feels like victory, and it feels like total freedom."

"Indeed," responded the Arcturian. "It IS freedom. You are creating total freedom from all indoctrinations that you received and believed during your many incarnations in the third-dimensional matrix. Close your eyes and see how the limitations of your third-dimensional indoctrinations are flowing away from your essence."

I did as the Arcturian asked and, for the first time, I truly realized the meaning of freedom. I was free of shackles I never knew I had. Life after life moved through my mind. One by one, those old energies of limitation were released.

Then I felt almost like my old, third-dimensional limitations came to me and thanked me for releasing them from the bondage of habit. It appears that before I could go to New Earth I would have to release ALL attachments to my own sorrow, suffering, and limitation.

Of course the only way that I could truly release these attachments was to deeply and totally feel them. With my conscious attention on releasing all the density that bonded me to the third dimension, I heard the Arcturian say, "Remember to transmute all third-dimensional limitations with the Violet Fire."

Yes, of course, the Violet Fire. I had to clean up all the darkness that I had created and gathered from all my many incarnations on Earth. I had forgotten that when I first came from the Starship and took a body here on Earth, I also took bodies in many different timelines.

It was my hope that by having incarnations on many different timelines I would learn more about being a third-dimensional human on planet Earth. I did not realize then that in order to return to the fifth-dimension I would have to release *every* psychic "footprint" I had left on Gaia's body.

It was then that I slowly started to perceive the thought forms I had just created. In fact, I saw how my first thought forms were filled with all my suffering, anger, sorrow, and shame. I could also see how the unconditional love for my self was moving through every thought form, loving and forgiving all the third-dimensional limitations that had attached to my essence.

"Now," said the Arcturian. "See the Violet Fire of transmutation."

I remembered how, long ago, Mytria had instructed me to "jump into the Violet Fire." I remembered how it felt and how I felt when I was within it. I allowed myself to feel the Violet Fire flowing into every cell and atom of my physical shell.

I could feel my entire body become lighter and lighter as the density of my thoughts, feelings and physical form were released into the Violet Fire. Slowly I began to experience my self lifting up. However, my "SELF" was NOT a being of flesh and blood. My SELF was a being of Violet Light and Unconditional Love.

Dear Lisa, my beloved daughter, you were right. I am going to New Earth. In fact, I wrote this message into my computer via Bob's QBC.

~THE FAMILY~

"What," said the adults in one voice.

"I knew it," the children said together.

"Oh, the innocence of youth," Bruce responded to their comment.

Lisa was too busy crying from joy to say anything. Then Leslie and Sam both stood up and began to slowly walk across the room.

"Mommy, Daddy," Leslie and Sam said in one voice. "Look, there is the doorway! Do you see it," they continued as they ran towards it.

"Wait," said the adults as the children ran into the door. "Wait for us."

As the adults, including Joan's new boyfriend, literally ran toward the doorway to catch up with the children, they heard Leslie and Sam saying, "Hi, Grandma. We missed you."

"But how can you be here, Grandma? I thought that you were on the threshold of New Earth?" asked Sam with his innate wisdom and multidimensional thinking.

Beverly waited for everyone to gather around her before she answered Sam's astute question.

"Well, honey," Beverly said in an unconditionally loving way. "I am not where you are. You are where I am."

It was Lisa who first understood what her mother said. "Do you mean that we are on threshold New Earth and you are our instructor to guide us to the next octave?"

Lisa's question was answered as the illusion of their living room was released from the family's joined consciousness, and they found themselves in the most beautiful place they could imagine.

"How long has our reality on physical Earth been an illusion?" Bruce wisely asked.

"Always!" answered Beverly.

Made in the USA
Columbia, SC
22 January 2022